I WANT TO TELL YOU LOVE

 UNIVERSITY OF CALGARY Press

Milton Acorn and bill bissett

I want to tell you love

A CRITICAL EDITION

EDITED BY
Eric Schmaltz and Christopher Doody

© 2021 Eric Schmaltz and Christopher Doody

University of Calgary Press
2500 University Drive NW
Calgary, Alberta
Canada T2N 1N4
press.ucalgary.ca

All rights reserved.
No part of this book may be reproduced in any format whatsoever without prior written permission from the publisher, except for brief excerpts quoted in scholarship or review.

Permission to reprint poems by Milton Acorn granted by his estate.
The poems and illustrations by bill bissett are used with permission from the author/artist.
The following poems by Milton Acorn have been reprinted by permission of Mosaic Press, 1252 Speers Rd., Units 1 & 2, Oakville, ON L6L 5N9, www.mosaic-press.com from the book *In a Springtime Instant* originally published in 2012 and reprinted in 2015: Death Poem, Detail of a Cityscape, Does the Negro's Soft Voice, Girl, Poem ["Hair flowing yellow and still"], Poem ["My mother goes in slippers"], Poem for Sydney, Poem for the Astronauts, The Schooner, Self-Portrait, To Conceive of Tulips, Thunder Poem, Untitled ["Lover that I hope you are … Do you need me?"].

LIBRARY AND ARCHIVES CANADA CATALOGUING IN PUBLICATION

Title: I want to tell you love / Milton Acorn and bill bissett ; edited by Eric Schmaltz and Christopher Doody.
Names: Acorn, Milton, author. | Bissett, Bill, 1939- author. | Schmaltz, Eric, 1988- editor. | Doody, Christopher, 1986- editor.
Description: Critical edition. | Includes bibliographical references and index.
Identifiers: Canadiana (print) 20210217146 | Canadiana (ebook) 20210217197 | ISBN 9781773852294 (softcover) | ISBN 9781773852317 (PDF) | ISBN 9781773852324 (EPUB)
Subjects: LCSH: Acorn, Milton—Criticism and interpretation. | LCSH: Bissett, Bill, 1939-—Criticism and interpretation. | CSH: Canadian poetry (English)—20th century—History and criticism. | LCGFT: Poetry.
Classification: LCC PS8501.C8 I9 2021 | DDC C811/.54—dc23

The University of Calgary Press acknowledges the support of the Government of Alberta through the Alberta Media Fund for our publications. We acknowledge the financial support of the Government of Canada. We acknowledge the financial support of the Canada Council for the Arts for our publishing program.

Copyediting by Brian Scrivener
Cover design, page design, and typesetting by Melina Cusano

Contents

Critical Introduction by Eric Schmaltz | 1
Influences and Self-Definitions | 6
The Vancouver Sixties Poetic Milieu | 11
In Vancouver: Milton Acorn and bill bissett | 18
A Textual History | 30
Thinking in Mosaics | 34
Afterlives | 52
Notes | 54
Bibliography | 61

I Want to Tell You Love by Milton Acorn and bill bissett | 67

Afterword by bill bissett | 187

dissimilar apertures uv consciousness:
An Interview with bill bissett | 191

"Th Caruso Pome" by bill bissett | 201

Editorial Rationale | 213

Explanatory Notes | 215

Editors' Emendations | 229

Later Publication and Emendation List | 231

Index of Poems by Title | 245

Acknowledgements | 249

Index | 251

Critical Introduction

Eric Schmaltz

"Lover that I hope you are . . . Do you need me?"

—Milton Acorn

I Want to Tell You Love documents the significant, but little known, collaboration between two of Canada's most illustrious and controversial literary icons as they navigated the broad social and political turbulence of the 1960s. Soon after they met in Vancouver, avant-garde poet and painter bill bissett and working-class People's Poet Milton Acorn combined their seemingly incongruous poetics to present a vision of resistance and transformation they titled *I Want to Tell You Love*. The book is composed of words and images: thirty-nine poems by Acorn, twenty-two poems by bissett, and ten drawings by bissett. Each of their contributions is distinctive and compelling, and some of these poems will be familiar to readers acquainted with the authors. However, when joined in this dialogic context, the significance and meaning of many of these poems is renewed and consequently revised. Their collaboration confronts a historical moment of instability, stimulated by broad social changes around the globe and the well-spring of utopian ideals known as the North American counterculture movement. When they met, bissett and Acorn were enmeshed within a series of social and political movements and events at home and abroad, including responses to the ravages of the Vietnam War, the Quiet Revolution's 1960 call for cultural secularism, the 1962 Cuban Missile Crisis, the 1963 assassination of United States President John F. Kennedy, the rise of the Civil Rights Movement, and the spectre of nuclear war. Concomitantly, these urgent episodes were complemented by countercultural activities, which prompted a revolution in social norms that altered the cultural fabric of North American life, including its music, dress, sexuality, family values, and attitudes toward drug use. These revolutionary stirrings figure as both a response to the social and political changes underway as well as a reaction against the culture of conformism that dominated North America in the 1950s. Acorn and bissett, then, in a few words, were working together during a turbulent period, characterized by the promise of an emergent culture and the seeming threat of the Cold War. The complexity of this moment and the vitality of the 1960s manifest in *I Want to Tell You Love*.

In its intended form as a collaborative book, *I Want to Tell You Love* has never been published until now.[1] In the past, editors and publishers were unable to see the congruities between the authors that exist across the book, which now seem like an almost logical partnership. Acorn and bissett submitted *I Want to Tell You Love* to several publishers, including Raymond Souster at Contact Press and Fred Cogswell at *Fiddlehead*—all of whom rejected the submission for one reason or another (see "A Textual History"). The most illuminative rejection notice was sent to Acorn on 28 March 1966 by J. A. Rankin, Editor of Trade Books for McClelland and Stewart (M&S). In her letter, Rankin reports that M&S's readers enjoyed many of the individual poems; however, they felt that the two styles of the poets "seem to oppose rather than complement each other."[2] Rankin and the readers at M&S were fundamentally correct. The styles of Acorn and bissett are dissimilar, but the poets already knew this: "There is more in common between me and, say, Baudelaire, then there is between you and me," writes Acorn to bissett in 1965.³

Acorn self-published his first slim collection of poems nine years earlier, *In Love and Anger* (1956) and, before meeting bissett, had already established a strong poetic voice that was characterized by conciseness in his language and imagery. Acorn's work from this early period of his career has "received praise for his handling of material in short lyrical poems" which offer "an immediate regional locale and marvellously sustained mood."⁴ His lengthier diatribes, some of which were to be published as part of *I Want to Tell You Love*, have been regarded by critics such as Shane Neilson as "awful polemics."⁵ bissett, on other hand, would soon publish his first books of poetry, *We Sleep Inside Each Other All* (1966) and *fires in th tempul OR th jinx ship nd othr trips* (1966), wherein we see the early emergence of bissett's unique orthography and his exploration of the radical possibilities afforded by misusing the typewriter, an aesthetic that would later be critically lauded by poet and critic Steve McCaffery for its "excess and libidinal flow"⁶ that stages an attempt to get "outside of writing"⁷—that is, to obliterate writerly conventions. Critics and poets such as Darren Wershler and Adeena Karasick have built upon or responded to McCaffery's analysis, consolidating it as a foundational characterization of bissett's poetics. *I Want to Tell You Love* is a remarkable opportunity to glimpse bissett's early career as he builds toward this recognizable aesthetic and given that bissett's first two books came out in 1966 (after Acorn and bissett completed work on the typescript), *I Want to Tell You Love* could have been bissett's first book of poetry, had it been published.⁸ *I Want to Tell You Love* presents evidence of Acorn's attempt to move beyond tight lyrical forms toward more sprawling and socially-focused poems. These noticeable differences in aesthetics were fundamental to M&S's decision. What the readers at M&S failed to appreciate, however, is that the disjunction created by their opposing aesthetics was precisely the point of their work.

Despite Acorn and bissett's eventual abandonment of *I Want to Tell You Love*, their collaboration remains an important document for their careers, literary reputations, and for the history of Canadian Literature. The typescript is not only evidence of a significant friendship and collaboration, but it also offers a look at the development of both authors' poetic voices and a glimpse at their contributions to Vancouver's emergent countercultural and radical literary communities. Many of the poems included in *I Want to Tell You Love* appeared later in independently produced volumes. While they are important works on their own—effectively representing their separate aesthetic orientations—the poems are renewed within a collaborative context. Scholar of the Canadian literary avant-garde Gregory Betts recognizes the significance of their collaboration when he briefly identifies the alliance between the aesthetic and radical political branches of the avant-garde within the work; he writes, "they recognized a parallel in Acorn's radical politics and bissett's radical formal experiments."[9] There are various modes of composition in *I Want to Tell You Love*, including pastoral lyrics, confessional lyrics, polemical diatribes, prose poems, and typographical experiments, but it is the authors' shared interest in radicalism that provides a provisional rationale for their collaboration. It is evident from seeing *I Want to Tell You Love* in this published form that their visions parallel each other in a most fundamental sense: literary radicalism with a belief in revolutionary possibility.

This first-ever published edition of *I Want to Tell You Love* is an opportunity to cast a backward glance at a momentous but momentary meeting in the lives of two of Canada's celebrated poets in the 1960s. Since then, both poets have enjoyed productive careers. After his days in Vancouver, and his frustrated efforts to publish *I Want to Tell You Love*, Acorn did not stop writing; in fact, he entered the most industrious period of his career and published more than five books. He was nominated for a Governor General's Award in 1970 for his book of poetry *I've Tasted My Blood* (1969). He did not win the award for this collection;

however, Canada's literary community celebrated his writing by giving him the title "The People's Poet," which came with a medal and monetary prize. Acorn would not be passed up again when he was nominated for a second Governor General's Award for his book *The Island Means Minago* (1975). While some critics have suggested that Acorn's fame has ebbed from national consciousness since his death in 1986, readers continue to enjoy his work, as recently demonstrated by Kent Martin and Errol Sharpe's 2015 compilation, *Milton Acorn: The People's Poet* (including a reprinted edition of *I've Tasted My Blood* with Acorn's handwritten notes). bissett's career also flourished after their collaboration. He published his first two full-length collections of poetry, *We Sleep Inside Each Other All* (1966) and *fires in th tempul OR th jinx ship nd othr trips* (1966), which conceptually could have been bissett's second and third books had *I Want to Tell You Love* been published.[10] bissett enjoyed a different path to notoriety, including accusations by Members of Parliament in the 1970s that he was publishing pornography with his *blewointment press*. These scandalous instances only contributed to bissett's profile as one of Canada's most radical poets, whose work has inspired critics and readers to generate a substantial body of criticism that engages his many publications—books, chapbooks, cassettes, compact discs, drawings, collages, and more. bissett, who now lives in Toronto, continues to write and paint.

This introduction will acquaint readers with *I Want to Tell You Love* along with the places, figures, and ideas that were central to the creation of the book. It begins by providing an overview of the tradition and milieu within which Acorn and bissett were writing in the 1960s. It then moves on to chronicle the convergence of events that led to their meeting in Vancouver. Next, it provides a detailed textual history of *I Want to Tell You Love*'s creation and its subsequent history of dismissal. Penultimately, it advances a short treatise that underscores the book's significance and its contributions to the discourse of Canadian Literature and the history of avant-garde writing. It concludes with a few points regarding bissett's and Acorn's careers and friendship after their time in Vancouver. Despite their aesthetic differences, bissett and Acorn both hold a fundamental belief in poetry's transformative capacities for stimulating social change. This edition fosters greater attention to *I Want to Tell You Love* as a significant meeting of discordant voices, but more importantly as a significant record of Canadian avant-garde activity that engages with, and documents, the frenzy and exhilaration of the 1960s in Canada.

Influences and Self-Definitions

Having met in the early 1960s, Acorn and bissett were acting in a moment that critics recognize as the beginning of Canada's cultural nationalist reawakening. In the wake of the Second World War, this was a period of decolonization that saw many British and French colonies working toward independence. Similarly, Canadians sought cultural independence and a distinguished identity. Canadian writers, for example, were undergoing intensive and contentious debates regarding self-definition, striving to determine their political future, and struggling against forces of influence from Britain and the United States. Canada had not yet realized itself as the "cultural mosaic," the official multicultural policy not implemented by the Canadian government until the 1970s and 1980s that it purports to be today. Recounting the shifts and developments underway for Canadians navigating the prospect of a national identity in the early 1960s, political scientist and philosopher Ron Dart writes that,

> The defeat of the Canadian Tory nationalist tradition of Prime Minister John Diefenbaker in 1963 by Lester Pearson and Tommy Douglas moved Canada in a political, economic, and military manner more toward the American orbit and gravitational field. U. S. President John F. Kennedy detested Diefenbaker and welcomed Pearson. George Grant's important publication *Lament for a Nation: The De-*

feat of Canadian Nationalism (1965) pondered the 1963 election and lamented the passing away of an older High Tory nationalism, but ignited a new generation of Canadian left-of-centre nationalists.[11]

Dart's summary of this moment highlights some notable shifts in Canada's political ethos that were deeply felt by Canadians. Famed Canadian children's author and poet Dennis Lee gives language to this moment with its a feeling of uncertainty, referring to it as a "form of civil alienation"[12] that presents a significant cultural problem for the nation's citizens: "if we live in a space which is radically in question for us, that makes our barest of speaking a problem to itself."[13] For Lee, the prospect of advancing a vision of national identity in cultural work is limited by pressures put on Canadians by external influences.

One of the central issues of debate regarding Canadian collective identity and cultural autonomy was the reignited desire to better define concepts like freedom, equality, and democracy in North America, which Canadian literary critics Laura Moss and Cynthia Sugars suggest had been hollowed out.[14] By the 1960s, a gap between the definitions of these words and the actual lived experience of them was apparent to North Americans. If freedom is the right to act, think, and speak as one desires, why were women, racial minorities, the disabled, and the poor denied equality and full autonomy within the existing social and political systems? As a result of unsatisfactory answers to these kinds of questions, the 1960s saw the rise of the Civil Rights movement—African Americans struggled for rights in the United States and Indigenous peoples demanded rights in Canada; women continued to fight against sexual inequality and repression; queer communities fought for rights despite potential criminal charges for their sexual orientation. These struggles were concurrent with and complemented by the waves of student strikes, sit-ins, and peace movements at colleges and universities instigated primarily by white "baby boomers" who were rejecting the repressive conformism of their upbringing in the 1950s. These youthful activists identified with Civil Rights struggles and set themselves in opposition to violent American occupations and invasions such as The Bay of Pigs Invasion (1961) and the Vietnam War (1955-75).

Many Canadians watched the failed efforts of the United States to fight Communism abroad. The Bay of Pigs Invasion involved a covertly funded group of Cuban exiles (backed by the United States) who attempted and failed to invade Cuba which was then governed by the Marxist-Leninist and Cuban nationalist Prime Minister Fidel Castro. Similarly, the War in Vietnam was another failed attempt to fight against Communism by the United States, which funded the South Vietnamese against the Soviet-funded North Vietnamese. This effort resulted in years of violent conflict and over a million deaths of both Americans and Vietnamese. Canada's youthful generation registered these events with horror and outrage. Canadians were beginning to view the United States as a country that hoped to become an imperial power, and this anxiety was heightened by the effects of the Cold War on home soil. Criticizing the United States's thirst for dominance, Canadian poet and activist Jamie Reid refers to the Cold War as a "North American form of fascism."[15] With the threat of the United States' Cold War efforts, along with the spectre of the horrific nuclear bombings in Nagasaki and Hiroshima, Reid recalls that Canadians of his generation, "lived every day and dreamed every night in fear that the city might actually be incinerated, the entire earth of people wasted and destroyed."[16] Though Canada did not actively support U.S. efforts in Vietnam on the ground, many Canadians felt the call to join the anti-war and pro-peace movement, thus signalling a greater resistance to American influence.[17]

The tensions felt in the 1960s were a more palpable and violent extension of the threat of U.S. dominance that Canadians felt as early as the 1950s. The findings of *The Massey Report: A Royal Commission on National Development in the Arts, Letters, and Sciences* (1951) claim that the ideological "price may be excessive" for cultural imports from the United States[18] and refer to the distribution of American films, radio programs, and periodicals as an "invasion" that "may stifle rather than stimulate our own creative effort."[19] The Canadian government eventually responded to these issues most forcefully at the end of the 1950s, pledging concerted financial support for the arts by establishing organizations like the Canada Council for the Arts. These strategic moves, along with the presage of global upheaval, gave rise to the nationalist sentiments that began to unfurl in the 1960s. Movements toward decolonization, the lingering effects of the Second World War, the U.S.-led violence in Vietnam and Latin America, Canada's resistance to U.S. imperialism, the loosening of ties to Britain, and a youthful and passionate generation of students and activists, all contributed to the perspectives of writers and artists who sought to define their nation during this time. Against this backdrop of high political and social tension, Canadian authors began to find their voice, and Canadian readers began to listen, finding glimpses of themselves in their novels, poems, and plays.

Among the many critics and authors who recognize the 1960s as a decisive period in the development of a Canadian literary national identity, Nick Mount recounts the efflorescent activities that he describes as a "literary explosion unlike anything Canada has ever experienced."[20] Mount more precisely identifies this period as the "long 1960s," beginning in 1959, two years after the first meeting of the newly founded Canada Council for the Arts, chaired by Brooke Claxton. Mount underscores 1959 as the beginning of this period because it saw the establishment of critical literary venues such as the University of British Columbia's journal *Canadian Literature* and the *Toronto Daily Star*'s book review column. These new forums made way for even more significant developments. In the ensuing years, Canada saw a rise of small literary reading series such as the readings held at coffee houses, including the Bohemian Embassy in Toronto. Canada also saw a significant increase in the number of Canadian-authored, Canadian-published English literary books, which occurred in step

Critical Introduction 9

with an explosion of book retailers across the country, indicating a surge in Canadian readers. A high watermark for the development of Canadian activity was the 1967 Canadian Centennial celebrations with Expo 67 in Montreal, which prominently featured the country's many cultural offerings. This exciting period of nationalist vigour, according to Mount, ends in approximately 1974 with the reification of a Canadian literary culture. By then, Northrop Frye had published his landmark essay "Conclusion to a *Literary History of Canada*" (1971); Margaret Atwood issued her 1972 treatise on what she believed was the central theme of Canadian Literature—"survival;" and her publisher, the poet Dennis Lee, regaled Canadians with poems of Canadian citizenship in *Civil Elegies* (1972) after regaining his voice that he believed was suppressed by British colonialism and American influence. These events, along with the establishment of The Writers' Union of Canada in 1973 and the Toronto Harbourfront Reading Series in 1974, are said to mark the "arrival" of a comprehensive Canadian literary culture that was concurrent with the establishment of a recognizable Canadian identity.

Mount's narrative for the development of Canadian literary identity is also a narrative of the arrival of the literary status quo and the establishment of a literary canon. It is a period during which Canadian audiences began to determine their literary tastes and inclinations, and those preferences would not have included *I Want to Tell You Love*. Mount's representation of the "CanLit Boom" touches on only some elements of Canada's unconventional literary underground and its radical literary practitioners. His narrative is a useful resource for readers seeking a sweeping overview of the establishment of Canadian literary hegemony in the mid-twentieth century; however, previous studies by scholars such as Pauline Butling remind readers of the profitability of attending to "local narratives of emergence"[21] in Canada's literary history. It is by looking at these local narratives, as Butling suggests, that readers often find the entanglement of geographic, personal, social, economic, and political forces that produce any given literature, including texts like *I Want to Tell You Love*.

The Vancouver Sixties Poetic Milieu

Vancouver is one of the Canadian cities where the "local narratives of emergence" are plentiful and varied. It is here that Canadians and American ex-pats in the 1960s actively explored the possibilities of nationalist self-definitions, the threat of American influence, the openings provided by liberationist attitudes in art and life, and the implications of new literary activities across the country. Remarking specifically on the year 1966, but capturing a sense of the times more broadly, Vancouver-based visual poet Judith Copithorne identifies this period as "without doubt, the best and worst of times," acknowledging that Vancouver in the 1960s was a site of many cooperative and oppositional forces.[22] It was a city stirred by the pursuit of liberated lifestyles, tense literary-political relations, and the horrors of global violence.

As a city located on the West Coast, thousands of miles away from the powerful centres of political and cultural life in Toronto and Ottawa, Vancouver felt to some as though it was excluded from the country's dominant poles. In an interview with Irene Niechoda and Tim Hunter, Frank Davey—who was a poet and student in Vancouver in the 1960s and is now an influential Canadian literary critic—recalls the compounding circumstances that led to this sense at the time. He writes,

> I think we felt marginalized in a number of ways, having come from a small town. Marginalized by being Canadian in North America, marginalized by being from the West Coast and British Columbian, in the Canadian context; marginalized by becoming more and more interested in language rather than in content, which was the dominant esthetic. That sense of being marginalized, and the

> anger that that aroused in us, was I think a very important source of the abrasive energy.[23]

Indeed, hardly disheartened by their geographical locale, poets and cultural workers were among the actors who transformed Vancouver into a vibrant Canadian literary outpost in which Acorn and bissett developed their collaboration.

One particularly rebellious group who helped to raise the profile of the city included Davey along with his peers Fred Wah, Jamie Reid, George Bowering, David Dawson, Daphne Buckle [Marlatt], Robert Hogg, and Gladys Hindmarch. They made themselves known as the TISH poets (an anagram of "shit"). They united their efforts in 1961 at the University of British Columbia (UBC) with the support of American expatriate professor Warren Tallman who introduced these then-aspiring poets to the rich, emerging tradition of American Beatnik and Black Mountain poetics. At the time, the university was primed for creative energizing. In 1959, well-established Canadian poet, novelist, and playwright Earle Birney created Canada's first Master of Fine Arts program in Creative Writing at UBC. Birney was among the poets living in Vancouver at the time, along with fellow committed leftists Pat Lowther and Dorothy Livesay (who shared ardent nationalist sentiments with Acorn) and Al Purdy, who were recognizable names to the Canadian literary mainstream in the 1960s. As Tallman recounts those days, he implies that the students in UBC's creative writing program desired a cultural and pedagogical shift away from Vancouver's current offerings. He writes that all students

> testified to his [Birney's] openness and generosity in responding to a Modernism he as poet happened not to prefer. He allowed them maximum freedom in class, write what and as you want. And he used his influence as one of Canada's leading poets to help them obtain assistance, grants, publication,

> the varieties of encouragement young poets need, praise not in departure, but at the outset.

However, "in forming a creative writing department at UBC, his eclecticism entered in as he, the least academic of men, let it be formed in the image of the academic world."[24] Tallman believed that the rigour of academic life at UBC was not compatible with creative labour. Recognizing this, Tallman sought to break the orthodoxy of creative culture at UBC.

Tallman introduced his students and, inadvertently or not, a broader community of writers to a nascent wave of American poetry and poetics as it was anthologized by Donald Allen in *The New American Poetry, 1945-1960* (1960). What began as a summer Sunday study group of recent poetry publications with Bowering, Davey, Dawson, Lionel Kearns, Reid, and Wah, flourished into a poetic ferment aligned with an American aesthetic ethos that drew from "modern jazz and abstract expressionist painting."[25] Instead of adhering to any kind of rigid academic schedule, Tallman introduced the community to poets such as Robert Duncan, Charles Olson, and Robert Creeley through workshops, class visits, reading groups, readings, and parties. These activities reached a high watermark in 1963 when Tallman and Creeley organized what is commonly referred to as the Vancouver Poetry Conference, which included American poets Duncan, Olson, Allen Ginsberg, Denise Levertov, Philip Whalen, and Canadian poet Margaret Avison. They convened in the city for an intensive three-week program related to poetry and poetics, featuring discussions, lectures, and readings. The 1963 meeting of poets, organized by Tallman, for which he "farmed in so many Americans,"[26] did much to define a contested poetic lineage in Canada that remains central to literary scholarship today. In particular, and given the anxiety many Canadians felt about the influence of American cultural exports on Canadian identity, Tallman's influence was polarizing, leading some poets, like Acorn, to rail against him and obliquely label him an agent of American cultural imperialism.[27]

Regardless, Reid writes in his posthumously published book *A Temporary Stranger* that the introduction of new American poets to Vancouver was indispensable to the development of Canadian poetry today and that "there never would have been any poetry of consequence in Vancouver, never any Vancouver poetry scene, without what Warren and Ellen Tallman did."[28]

Though Tallman sought to disrupt scholarly norms at UBC, the creative scene in the downtown exceeded his efforts to liberate creative life from academic rigour. Just as he mythologizes Tallman's influence, Reid also paints a vivid portrait of Vancouver's "hippie uprisings."[29] Away from the university, the culture of Vancouver's downtown creative class was spurred by the 1957 obscenity trial for Ginsberg's *Howl* and began to unfold with its newly opening Beatnik bars, clubs, and cafes such as the Cellar, Black Spot, and the Den.[30] Reid explains that in the sixties there were

> two centres of poetic activity in the city in earliest part of those days: one was at the University of British Columbia, centred around Warren Tallman and the group known as the TISH poets . . . The other was loosely centred around the Vancouver School of Art, and Jack Shadboldt might be considered its very distant professor—later, that group was to centre around bill bissett and his blewointment press on Fourth Avenue. Warren Tallman referred to this second group as the 'downtown poets,' though the designation was very loose.[31]

This latter group included Roy Kiyooka, Al Neil, Fred Douglas, Jock Hearn, Judith Copithorne, Maxine Gadd, and bissett. Much like the TISH poets, this group of artists extended Vancouver's reputation as an innovative locale in Canada's cultural history and did so by exploring intersectional possibilities that fused writing, music, dance, painting, and sculpture.

Unlike the TISH poets, the artists and poets of the downtown more fully embraced the liberationist spirit of the sixties counterculture with communal living, mind-altering drugs, political action (protests, sit-ins, be-ins), and other pursuits to escape middle class conformity. In her personal account of Vancouver's Sixties Generation, Copithorne notes the growing interest in cannabis and Eastern mysticism as well as the proliferation of left-leaning political philosophies, which prompted gatherings of socialist artists and activists at Vanguard Books at 1208 Granville Street.[32] This Beat-inspired culture was complemented by psychedelic dance parties and cross-disciplinary creative happenings, festivals, and events at artist-run galleries and spaces such as Intermedia, Motion Studio, and the Sound Gallery. The downtown artists came to their countercultural awakening through the work of artists and thinkers without caring much for the creation of a Canadian lineage or identity. They listened to Bob Dylan's folk and protest songs, internalized Marshall McLuhan's theories of the electric age, built the far-out geodesic designs of architect Buckminster Fuller, and embraced the teachings of philosopher Herbert Marcuse's writings and lectures on liberation. These activities were intertwined with political actions such as anti-war and peace movements, socialist meetings, and feminist activism. Copithorne underscores the overlap of art and politics in Vancouver, recalling that, "The writers and artists I met at readings and galleries, I would also meet at demonstrations and meetings."[33] Alongside much of this activity, bissett's publishing efforts with *blewointment* (discussed more below) were a staple within Vancouver's milieu. He dedicated much needed space to the "self-committed agents of the counter-cultural rebellion" that existed outside of the TISH circle that sought an even more radical vision of liberated art and life.[34]

Vancouver's creative and political vibrance has been well documented by critics, artists, and poets, who compellingly mythologize the city. They also present conflicting accounts of the many forces that converged as part of everyday lived experience.

Critically acclaimed literary biographer Christine Wiesenthal, in *The Half-Lives of Pat Lowther* (2005), presents a divided map of Vancouver's groups and personalities in the 1960s. For Wiesenthal, Vancouver was not only home to established leftist writers such as Lowther, Purdy, and Livesay, but also to a younger generation of poets, including bissett, Copithorne, and Gadd. Wiesenthal colourfully portrays the mentality that separated these groups; she writes, "Younger student radicals differed sharply from their elder 'comrades' in terms of their embrace of a more individualistic ethos, among other things. . . . The old guard, on the other hand . . . viewed the openly hedonistic, hippy, drop-out and drug crowds with suspicion and moral disdain that united it with the far right."[35] With her divisions between an older and younger generation of literary practitioners, Wiesenthal exemplifies the tensions in the city among its authors and intellectuals, highlighting the diverse values that underwrite the scene.

Alternately, some authors have presented contrasting narratives regarding Vancouver's various scenes that do not lean on hard separations between groups; rather, they identify the many ways these scenes overlap. Copithorne's personal account and checklist, for example, highlights the major personalities that affected her early creative life—Kenneth Patchen who read at Vancouver's The Cellar, accompanied by jazz musician Al Neil and his trio; artist and professor Roy Kiyooka, whom she met often at the Little Heidelberg Coffeehouse; and Helen Goodwin, whom she recognizes as a mentor to young women through dance classes at UBC and later Motion Studio.[36] Copithorne explains how she moved from jazz clubs to cafés to studios to protests where she met with artists, dancers, and activists across Vancouver's many factions. Copithorne's personal experience was not singular. Poet and musician Michael Turner offers a similarly convergent model of Vancouver's artistic communities that diminishes the distinction between the UBC TISH group and the downtown crowd[37] that Reid, echoing Tallman, positions in his narratives. There was indeed crossover between the groups. For example, by just looking at the names of featured poets in *TISH* and *blewointment*, it is clear that they were publishing each other to some extent. Regardless of how poets explain their lived experiences of Vancouver in the 1960s or how critics attempt to make sense of Vancouver's literary vibrance, it is not only the retrospective framework that makes Vancouver a compelling literary location. Rather, it is all these forces working together simultaneously that gives the city its iconic status as a touchstone of creative exploration and sociopolitical action.

Acorn and bissett shared a unique relationship to Vancouver's dynamic scene. They were both outsider poets—literally, since they were both born in Canada's maritime provinces, but also because their creative orientations did not tidily align with any one of Vancouver's factions. As indicated by his disdain for academics and American poetics, Acorn was repelled by the creative happenings at UBC. One would expect that Acorn would arrive in Vancouver and find close companionship with writers like Livesay and Lowther—and he did. Yet, he also circulated among Vancouver's other groups and spent much of his time with the younger countercultural poets like bissett. He was discontented with the politics of Vancouver and ensured, as discussed below, there were more outlets for political discussion by organizing reading nights and co-founding the counterculture newspaper *The Georgia Straight*. Likewise, bissett also found some initial difficulty in establishing himself as part of Vancouver's creative life. Like Acorn, he was uninterested in academics, and he gravitated instead toward the downtown's more capacious lifestyle of drugs, cafés, and happenings. bissett, however, was not quite satisfied with simply fitting in; thus, he inserted himself as a force within the downtown scene, breaking down disciplinary walls by fusing his poetic with visual and performance art. He started *blewointment* with a few likeminded poet-friends to showcase this kind of work—concrete poetry, sound poetry, and other genre-bending poetries—because until then it was being ignored.[38] With *blewointment*, bissett began to create his own community and signal boost the culture of the city that was being left out. Acorn and bissett were an unlikely pair who found themselves unlike many of the other poets in the city. However, they were alike in that they were cultural figures who sought to open poetic and political opportunities wherever they saw the need.

In Vancouver: Milton Acorn and bill bissett

Acorn and bissett discretely arrived in Vancouver amid this unfurling of creative and political vitalities—bissett in 1958 and Acorn in 1963. They first became acquainted at a meeting for the League of Socialist Action held at Vanguard Books. Ruth Bullock, a long-time activist and the owner of the radical Marxist hangout, introduced them to each other, and there they bonded over a shared interest in poetry and ongoing sociopolitical affairs. Surprisingly, there is nothing, according to bissett, that the two disagreed on. This seeming compatibility is surprising since Acorn was a notoriously difficult companion. Recounting their friendship, Purdy remembers that he and Acorn "used to disagree on practically everything," and he notes, too, that Acorn had a similar relationship with poet and songwriter Leonard Cohen.[39] Perhaps what distinguishes bissett from Cohen and Purdy, in this respect, is that Acorn and bissett shared a great deal—they were both poets with leftist political leanings, committed to controlling the production of literature with their magazines, and believed in the possibility of creating a better and more equitable world. Acorn and bissett also shared a similar relationship to Vancouver. Neither poet was a native Vancouverite, and both had come there from Canada's eastern coast to insert themselves as central personalities in the West Coast scene.

As it is well-documented by Ed Jewinski (1991), Chris Gudgeon (1996), Richard Lemm (1999), and others, Acorn is renowned as a blustery literary figure in Canada. Notoriously difficult to get along with, he was strong minded, mercurial, and politically charged. He held idiosyncratic views that he believed folded together Marxist, Leninist, Trotskyist, Maoist, and Canadian nationalist positions.[40] As he built this reputation, he spent much of his writing career circulating among Canada's literary metropolises—Montreal, Toronto, and Vancouver. Acorn was born in Charlottetown, Prince Edward Island in 1923, where he lived until sometime between 1950 and 1951, when he moved to Montreal. Acorn's relocation marked the beginning of his more serious commitment to poetry as well as the pattern of migration that would guide much of his writing life as he moved between provinces. He had previously worked as a carpenter with strong aspirations for poetry, and he fully committed himself to the latter task when he reportedly, with Purdy at his side, sold his carpentry tools at a shop in Montreal in 1956.[41] After Montreal, he moved to Toronto for a time, where he continued to build his reputation, publishing his first full-length book *The Brain's the Target* in Toronto with Ryerson Press.

Acorn's period in Toronto is notably distinguished by his involvement with Toronto's coffeehouse Bohemian Embassy and, among other things, his vexed relationship with the exceptional poet Gwendolyn MacEwen. Soon after the Embassy opened, Acorn, according to literary biographer Rosemary Sullivan, "marched in and took it over, as if it had been especially created for him."[42] As he was known to do, he spent his time at the Embassy where he "drank hard and played hard"[43] while talking poetry and politics. His presence there was an early indication of his attraction to the counterculture and predilection to be located amidst cultural excitement. It was at the Embassy that Acorn met MacEwen, and where they developed a deep friendship and intimate bond grounded in poetry and poetics. Despite her frequent rebuffs of his advances, Acorn was persistent in pursuing MacEwen beyond friendship and persistently asked her to marry him. Eventually, MacEwen relented and, to the surprise, cynicism, and shock of their friends and community, they married on 8 February 1962. She was nineteen years old; Acorn was thirty-seven. Sullivan explains MacEwen's decision to marry Acorn as "humanly simple" and that "He was one of the few people who could touch her in profound isolation—an arm, a voice."[44] He was a person she missed when she was alone.

Acorn and MacEwen's short partnership unfortunately contributed to the harrowing conditions of their often turbulent lives. (They officially divorced in 1966.) Soon after their marriage, they moved to Ward's Island in the Toronto Harbour. Purdy visited them there and remembered "the enormous contrast between them."[45] These differences are illustrated, for example, by their decision to enjoy an open marriage. Though they agreed to be flexible with fidelity, "the thought of other lovers for Gwen, of course, sent Milton into a rage."[46] Fiercely independent, MacEwen left for Israel and returned with her mind made up to leave him. Acorn decided to do the same and boarded a train to Canada's West Coast before their marriage could be officially dissolved. It seemed as though Acorn's flirtations with liberated attitudes embedded in counterculture lifestyles in Toronto were not what he ultimately desired. The prospect of revolution and liberation was out there for Acorn, but he did not find it in Toronto nor with MacEwen. He was actually "deeply conservative and family values were important" to him, writes Sullivan.[47] According to her account of this phase in MacEwen's life, it was these irreconcilable parts of Acorn's personality—between radical poetry persona and conservative family man—that was majorly divisive in their relationship and drove him toward the West Coast where he would try to hold court among poets and activists of Vancouver's counterculture.

With his relationship to MacEwen nearly behind him, Acorn arrived in Vancouver in 1963. By this time, he had published *In Love and Anger* (1956) and *The Brain's the Target* (1960), one broadside entitled *Against a League of Liars* (1960), two full-length poetry books, the second of which, *Jawbreakers* (1963), came out during his transition year; and a special issue of *Fiddlehead* magazine was also dedicated to his work (1963). Leading up to this time, too, he had been co-editing and publishing the literary magazine *Moment* for several years, first with Purdy and then with MacEwen. Acorn's years in Toronto, and his relationship to MacEwen, may tint the lens we use to look at Acorn's conception of love;[48] however, they also mark the beginning of Acorn's earnest relationship with countercultural poets. Had it been published, *I Want to Tell You Love* would have been a significant intervention into Acorn's seemingly quiet period from 1964 to 1969.

In his biography, Lemm notes that Acorn arrived in Vancouver at a time of "lively poetic beginnings"[49] composed of multiple generations and a mix political and poetical factions. Though he often spurned American poets on account of his anti-academic bias (many of these poets were in Vancouver to visit with students at UBC), he threw himself into the city's poetic effervescence. He found kinship with a number of poets and communities, regardless of their age, career position, and political leanings. He befriended the young Red Lane, regarded as one of the most talented emerging poets in Vancouver in the early 1960s, as well as poet Patrick Lane (Red Lane's older brother and an esteemed poet in his own right).[50] Another close literary friendship that Acorn cultivated during this time was with poet Pat Lowther, with whom he lived for two months in 1968. In Lowther, he found both poetic and political compatibility; she was not only a well-respected poet, but she was devoted to socialist politics.

Acorn's friendships, among many others, were complemented by his direct work with the literary community. From 1963 to 1965, Acorn was the principal organizer for a reading series at Vanguard Books, and from 1964 until 1968, the principle organizer of a series at the Advance Mattress Coffee House, where he also created forums for political discussion known as the "Thursday night open-mike 'Blab sessions'."[51] He co-founded *The Georgia Straight* with Dan McLeod, Pierre Coupey, and Stan Persky in 1967. The magazine started as a response to the *Vancouver Sun*, which "mounted a campaign against the youth culture, 'Hippies,' and 'drug use'."[52] *The Georgia Straight*, in part, was meant to represent the youth community and "to expose and resist this harassment and misinformation."[53] Though there are competing accounts of Acorn's involvement with the paper's founding, Pierre Coupey claims that Acorn provided essential financial support in the sum of two hundred dollars to print the first issue.[54] He also served as a contributing editor in those early days. Through these activities, roles, and friendships, Acorn situated himself deeply within Vancouver, becoming central to its burgeoning creative and political culture.

In 1968, Acorn returned briefly to Toronto, then to Prince Edward Island. During the five years that he lived in Vancouver, he did not publish any chapbooks or full-length collections of poems, though he tried with *I Want to Tell You Love*. He left Vancouver and found tremendous success. In the year following his departure, 1969, Acorn broke his period of silence with his pivotal book of poems, *I've Tasted My Blood*, edited and introduced by Purdy. The quality of this collection was recognized by Canadians, earning Acorn a nomination for the 1970 Governor General's Award. The 1970 deliberation was contentious. It symbolized a major divide between nationalist and post-nationalist positions within Canada's literary community. Acorn was nominated with literary rival Bowering as well as his former partner MacEwen; Tallman was one of the judges for the award. This nomination folded together Acorn's disputation of American-influenced West Coast TISH poets and his turbulent marriage. Acorn was ultimately passed up for the award; Bowering and MacEwen shared it. The literary community responded in outrage and decried the decision because Tallman was on the award committee. By 1970, and in the wake of the Centennial Celebrations of 1967, Canadians were enjoying their nationalist surge, a position that led many Canadian authors to protest Tallman's involvement for his American identity. Rallying against the competition's results, Canadian authors across the country, led by poets Eli Mandel and Irving Layton, raised a sum of one thousand dollars. Supporters included Atwood, Purdy, Lane, and Mordecai Richler, among others. Along with the sum of money they invented a poetry prize, popularly known as the People's Poetry Prize, and awarded Acorn with both a medal and the fundraised money at Toronto's legendary Grossman's Tavern on 16 May 1970. More than one hundred friends and admirers of Acorn gathered at the tavern to honour Acorn, including Atwood, Layton, Mandel, Livesay, Purdy, Joe Rosenblatt, Douglas Fetherling, Graeme Gibson, and others. The gathering at Grossman's was as much a celebration of Acorn as it was of Canadian literary identity.

The 1970 award seemed to colour Acorn's perspective on Vancouver, bringing out the more combative side of his personality, especially regarding the relationship between poetry and nationalism. In 1972, Acorn published a short essay, "AVOID THE BAD MOUNTAIN," in *Blackfish* that directly attacks fixtures within the Vancouver scene, mainly the TISH poets. He acknowledges that TISH was one of the initial groups that attracted him to the city; he writes, "In spite of my repugnance, I was curious, and journeyed all the way to Vancouver on the conviction that where there was shit there must be animals."[55] However, he ungenerously attacks their work and fortifies the perception that the city's literary scene was divided; he writes, "I found a fascinating group of downtown poets whom the Tishites were trying to put down, by inventing an impossible set of rules."[56] Acorn continues in the essay to lambaste TISH and the influence they drew from the Black Mountain school (which he refers to as "Bad Mountain"). In response to what he sees as the deficiencies of TISH and Black Mountain poetics, he issues his own somewhat convoluted rules for poetry, which include the following: First, and contradictorily, avoid confining poetry with rules without totally ignoring the rules of poetry; second, do not limit subject matter for poetry, including political subject matter; third, avoid American models, especially Black Mountain, but he notes that Leroi Jones (later Amiri Baraka) is "sometimes very good"; fourth, use concise imagery; and, fifth, do not found schools of poetry like TISH.[57] Acorn even briefly extends his anti-Americanist argument to comment on bissett's poetry, praising bissett's poem "Th Canadian" and its critique of class but expressing disappointment with bissett's poems that he believes are influenced by Black Mountain poetics. This essay appears to be an opportunity for Acorn to lean into his persona as a Canadian nationalist, an especially significant gesture in the wake of the 1970 award debacle. In 1965, however, when they were collaborating on *I Want to Tell You Love*, Acorn seemed hardly disapproving of bissett's work nor of the scene being cultivated in Vancouver. It is, after all, what attracted him to Vancouver in the first place.

Like Acorn, bissett's life is patterned by restless movement, which also brought him to Vancouver for a major portion of his early creative life. bissett's first stop, before eventually settling in Toronto, was Vancouver. Sixteen years after Acorn, bissett was born in Halifax, Nova Scotia, in 1939 into a middle-class family with a lifestyle he routinely tried to escape. There are competing accounts of the timing of bissett's departure from the east coast. However, according to bissett, he finally escaped his middle-class station, and its sexual repression (bissett was openly bisexual in the 1960s), when he hitchhiked across Canada to Vancouver in the summer of 1958.[58] There, he attended UBC for two years, completing courses in English and Political Philosophy with professors such as Tallman and Birney and had no interest in other academic streams. bissett dropped out before he received his degree.

When bissett arrived in Vancouver, he undoubtedly found a sense of affinity with comradely leftist poets such as Lowther, and his youthfulness and penchant for experimentation were matched by the rebellious creativity of the TISH poets. Despite the consonance of their creative spirits, bissett—like Acorn—rejected the academic affinities of TISH. bissett's poetry and lifestyle distinguished him as a wild Bohemian and a Beatnik, which qualified him as a member of the downtown poets. He spent his early days painting and drawing as an outsider figure, a position that is confirmed in Canadian Broadcast Corporation's documentary *Strange Grey Day This* (1965). Comprising black-and-white camera shots of bissett moving through the city, his overdubbed voice describes the sense of animosity others felt for him. He was physically assaulted while walking on the street, which he believes was likely due to his comportment and clothing representative of the Beatnik lifestyle. He explains that people who resent Beatniks resent them for their sense of freedom. It is this sense of freedom—in both life and art—that defines bissett's career and reputation as one of Canada's most notorious convention-breaking and genre-bending poets and artists.

He spent these days with his former partner Martina Clinton and friend Lance Farrell—two of Vancouver's overlooked literary personalities. They were painting, writing, and cultivating their place in the scene. Looking back on this period in 2007, bissett says that they were "embraysing that sylabuls onlee mostlee n totalee eschewing th narrativ line 4 a mor xcellent sylabik uttrans writing n using th space uv th papr th page 2 avoid squares or rektanguls as th onlee shapes wun cud write in."[59] This early rejection of margins, straight lines, and the rectangular shape of the page is among the reasons that bissett is most frequently celebrated. By the mid- to-late 1960s, this impulse had culminated in a hybrid poetic—an expansive practice that does not distinguish poetry from sculpture, collage, drawing, music, or other art forms. However, when bissett had met Acorn, he had not quite arrived at this purview.[60] Unable to find a public outlet for his developing aesthetic, bissett began his own magazine in 1963, the infamously unconventional *blewointment* while bissett lived on Fleming Street in Vancouver.[61] In this way, Acorn and bissett shared a desire to control the means of literary production (as Acorn did with *Moment*) and were committed to providing public forums for writers.

Characterized by creative risk-taking activities, *blewointment* allowed bissett to publish his own poetry alongside like-minded peers, including Farrell, Clinton, Copithorne, and bpNichol. The magazine featured foundational forays into literary avant-gardism in Canada and welcomed a range of poetic styles—concrete poetry, lyric poetry, pattern poetry, collages, drawings, found materials, and more—and with a remarkable roster of writers, including Acorn, Atwood, Bowering, Purdy, Birney, Avison, Livesay, Lowther, Michael Ondaatje, Kiyooka, McCaffery, Nichol, and others. With each new issue, *blewointment* pushed boundaries including national boundaries by featuring an international array of poets such as d. a. levy, Diane di Prima, and Richard Kostelanetz (United States); Ivo Vroom (Belgium); Pierre Albert-Birot (France); Bob Cobbing (England); and others. With *blewointment*, bissett established himself as one of the city's most recognizable literary personalities, which eventually led to his first full-length poetry books, *We Sleep Inside Each Other All* and *Th jinx ship*.

bissett was known, too, for his psychedelically-influenced and avant-garde performances and exhibitions such as his work with Joy Long and Gregg Simpson as part of the Mandan Ghetto, a multipurpose artist space on West Fourth Avenue that they took over in 1968. As Simpson recalls, the space held "interesting exhibitions during the several months the gallery remained active, including the first show of surrealist collages ever held in Vancouver" which featured work by bissett, Long, Simpson, Ardis Breeze, Gary Lee Nova, and Ian Wallace.[62] The Mandan Ghetto also later hosted an important exhibition of sound and visual poetry, *Brazilia 73* (1973), which featured work by bissett, Coupey, Nichol, Gerry Gilbert, David W. Harris (also known as David UU), and Stephen Scobie with international contributions from levy, Henri Chopin, Ian Hamilton Finlay, Dom Sylvester Houédard, and Ernst Jandl. With these events and publication endeavours, bissett's reputation exceeded the city limits of Vancouver. In fact, in 1968, well-known Beatnik writer Jack Kerouac once remarked in an interview with poet Ted Berrigan for *The Paris Review* that bissett was a "great poet."[63]

bissett's centrality to Vancouver's counterculture also led to hardship and garnered some unwanted attention. bissett lived in poverty for much of his time in Vancouver—living in the 1960s, for example, in derelict housing in Vancouver with Clinton and their child. In addition to the harassment he faced on the street, he was assaulted in bars and clubs while performing his poetry.

Reid recounts seeing bissett perform at Vancouver's legendary jazz club The Cellar; he writes,

> bill that night was perched unsteadily on a narrow, wobbling formica table, looking ragged and vulnerable, reading his poems in a breathless, high, feminine voice. The place was filled with drunk and hateful males, men in their thirties and forties, who began yelling the worst insults they knew, inspired by their deepest homophobic fears: "Fruit!" "Queer!" "Fairy!" They began throwing things. A piece of crockery struck bill's cheekbone, drawing a drop of blood. By a kind of fatal synchronicity, the next line of bill's poem was 'I want to kill you!'[64]

The moment is demonstrative of the kind of discrimination bissett faced as well as his perseverance. bissett's tenacity was also unfortunately tested by the police, who routinely harassed him for his reputation as a "Hippie" and drug user. He was incarcerated for drug use on numerous occasions,[65] and in "1968, bissett was busted while taking marijuana to a Powell River commune. He spent several weeks at the Oakalla prison farm, plus some time in jail in Powell River, Vancouver, and Burnaby. He was fined $500. Federal authorities vowed to appeal the ruling, wanting a stiffer sentence."[66] Though these were undoubtedly taxing experiences, they contributed to bissett's purview. His work and commitment to alternative ways of being, even when they caused him strife, demonstrate his keen hope for a better world. Reid affectionately remarks on bissett, noting that "It is all only experience to him, his constant effort being always to make two different worlds cohere: the world of ordinary daily grime and ugliness, of 'real life' and hardship on one hand and the inner, celestial, spiritual world of sunshine and flowers on the other hand."[67] bissett's sense of radical individualism with his countercultural reputation and tireless optimism undoubtedly attracted Acorn.

bissett first met Acorn at Vanguard Books in 1964. They quickly developed a resonant friendship that revolved around poetry, politics, and publishing. At that time, bissett was gaining unwanted attention as an advocate for the legalization of marijuana and needed to get out of the spotlight. Following the recommendation of his friends, probation officer, and other local law enforcement, bissett, Clinton, and their daughter Michelle (then named Ooljah) left Vancouver for most of the winter of 1965 and traveled through California, Arizona, and Mexico. Acorn bought a painting from bissett—bissett's first painting sale, in fact—about a month before they left for the trip. bissett recalls that he was in Tucson, Arizona when Malcolm X was assasinated on 21 February 1965 and that he returned to Vancouver sometime in late March or early-to-mid April 1965. Acorn and bissett began work on *I Want to Tell You Love* when bissett returned.[68]

bissett looks back on his relationship with Acorn with great fondness. bissett recalls that, "he was a great carpentr n a great poet i liked him veree much n cud reelee groov with him . . . milton n me wud talk 4 hours n hours n walk n talk n talk n walk."[69] He remembers Acorn, like so many others, puffing endlessly on his cigar. Identifying their aligned political visions, Jewinski notes a rather comic instance wherein Acorn and bissett demonstrate their commitment to anti-Americanist and leftist politics by fundraising "$48 and, as Acorn put it, mailed the money to one of the Trotskyist factions, not really having any sense of what to do with the cash once they had raised it."[70] Patrick Lane recollects that Acorn was a vital presence in bissett and Clinton's home in the 1960s, alluding to a deep bond between Acorn and bissett's family. He recalls Acorn aiding in the collation of *blewointment* and that Michelle would frequently refer to Acorn as "Uncle Miltie."[71] bissett featured Acorn's writing in a number of issues of *blewointment*, beginning with the second issue in 1963 right until the penultimate issue, *What Isint Tantrik Speshul* in 1973.

Acorn, who at the time was a more established poet than bissett, helped bissett access a broader reading public. He gave bissett opportunities to read at Vanguard Books and Advance Mattress Coffee House, where Acorn organized events.[72] Acorn facilitated the publication of bissett's poetry in the March 1965 issue of long-running leftist magazine *Canadian Forum*—one of the most desired publication forums for emerging poets, which was edited by influential figures such as Northrop Frye and Milton Wilson. *Canadian Forum* featured bissett's "The Body" alongside writings by Alden Nowlan, Margaret Avison, and John Robert Colombo. This gave bissett both exposure to a more easterly audience and placed him among an established writerly company. These are significant gestures for an artist early in his career. bissett admits that his involvement with Acorn was "a veree important part uv th road uv my poetree development."[73]

With that said, this was not a typical story of mentorship between an established and emerging poet. Acorn felt that he had learned a great deal from bissett. On 27 December 1965, Acorn wrote to bissett:

> I have been reading over the typescript of "I Want to Tell You Love" . . . and for the first time I got a real sense of what terrifically good poetry you do write. Do you mind a confession? Certain things you said in certain poems impressed me terrifically. Certain whole poems impressed me terrifically . . . And yet I was tremendously unsure at every step of the composition of the typescript. My decision to bring out a book with you was influenced just as much by all I had observed about you . . . Your whole attitude to life. And then to a certain conviction of mine . . . that the young are the real ancients, they are older and wiser because they are born later, into an older

and wiser time . . . And this is particularly true of the gap between your generation and mine.⁷⁴

While they worked on *I Want to Tell You Love*, bissett was rapidly driving toward his multifaceted poetic voice, characterized by chanting and phonetic spelling. According to Tallman, it was around this time—in 1966—that bissett arrived at this poetic signature. bissett's movement toward this style in *I Want to Tell You Love* is evident, but especially when comparing changes made to some of his poems as they were written for this venture and his later publications. Through his collaboration with bissett, Acorn seems to have learned to appreciate the affordances of some avant-garde literary forms. Though he did not fully indulge the same impulse in his writing, the December 27ᵗʰ letter to bissett indicates that Acorn recognized and appreciated the emergence of a new wave and generation of writers distinct from his own. These distinctions were both the most striking features of their collaboration, but also—as indicated by Canadian editors—its most poignant hindrance.

A Textual History

As evidenced by their correspondence, Acorn and bissett completed their work for *I Want to Tell You Love* before 27 December 1965 (though it could have been much earlier). On that day, Acorn wrote a letter (cited above) to bissett, reminiscing about the typescript. bissett recalls that they began working on the typescript sometime earlier that same year, after returning from his trip through California, Arizona, Nevada, and Mexico. He remembers that, "me n my family i was part uv livd veree cheeplee in a hous that was being torn down."⁷⁵ At first, Acorn asked bissett to provide illustrations for a book of poetry that would have solely featured Acorn's poetry. This was not uncommon for Acorn. His first book of poems, *In Love and Anger* (1956), featured nearly a dozen illustrations by Montreal visual artist Robert Roussil. However, when it came time to create *I Want to Tell You Love*, Acorn encouraged bissett to become an equal partner in collaboration. This decision to invite bissett to collaborate on the book with him is what generated *I Want to Tell You Love*'s most striking qualities, but it is also what led to the exclusion of this work from the Canadian literary canon.

Rankin and M&S's decision not to publish *I Want to Tell You Love* was echoed by other editors and publishers in Canada. In the Afterword to this edition, bissett recalls that the book was routinely rejected because "nowun wud publish as our writing approaches wer sew diffrent peopul sd we cudint b in th same book that was th point ... i wud say 2 peopul sheesh."[76] Notes on *I Want to Tell You Love* held in The Very Stone House series of Seymour Mayne's archive at Library and Archives Canada (LAC) assist to contextualize some of *I Want to Tell You Love*'s history. These notes, which explicitly reference *I Want to Tell You Love*, were made for a selected volume of Acorn's poems that was in preparation for Very Stone House in the Spring of 1967. It seems highly likely, according to the numerous lists of poem titles, that they were editing *I Want to Tell You Love* into a single-authored book, consisting only of Acorn's poems. These selections and revisions took place in March and April of 1967. Like *I Want to Tell You Love*, this book was never published. It is unclear from the notes if a final selection of poems was made, but Acorn had already typed a candid and anecdotal Introduction for the book, which captures some of the misgivings he had for Vancouver as well as some publishers and fellow poets at the time. It details some now well-known resentment Acorn had for certain poets such as Bowering; however, this introduction offers some crucial details regarding *I Want to Tell You Love*'s history of dismissal.

As part of his bibliographic history in the introduction to the planned Very Stone House book, Acorn includes a note on his collaboration with bissett. Here, he identifies that the collaboration began when bissett offered to illustrate a book of his, but as Acorn claims, he "went him one better."[77] Thus, they decided to bring out a book together, consisting of poems from both authors and illustrations by bissett. Acorn also suggests that he selected which poems by bissett would be included in the book. This point has not been corroborated definitively by bissett. According to Acorn, "Everybody who's looked at the manuscript thought it was a lovely thing. Everybody but the publishers... (rejections)."[78] The publishers named by Acorn in this introduction do not include Rankin at M&S, whose notice of rejection was issued a full year (28 March 1966) before work on the Very Stone House book began. Acorn does, however, mention two publishers—Fred Cogswell at Fiddlehead Press and, in a more oblique reference, the acclaimed poet and publisher Raymond Souster at Contact Press, which Acorn diminishingly refers to as "Look-Maw-I'm-Modern-Press."[79]

According to Acorn, Cogswell, who had previously published a special issue of *Fiddlehead* magazine dedicated to Acorn's poetry in 1963, wanted to publish *I Want to Tell You Love*. Cogswell was unable to do so at the time because, as Acorn bluntly puts it, he "was stoney broke."[80] Souster's rejection of *I Want to Tell You Love* was evidently more agonizing for Acorn, since the pair had been close friends. Surprisingly, and perhaps in a mere fit of opinionated anger, Acorn here briefly rails against the press, suggesting that the book was rejected with deliberate malice. As bissett also recounts in his Afterword to this edition, we—bissett and myself—had the opportunity to visit Souster in 2012, just prior to his unfortunate death in the fall of that year. We shared a lovely afternoon with Souster—listening to Dixieland Jazz—and he gave us copies of his book *Easy Does It* (2011). Souster and bissett reminisced about past encounters at meetings for the League of Canadian Poets and shared touching and vivid memories of Acorn. When we came around to the topic of *I Want to Tell You Love*, Souster said he had no recollection of the book. That absence reverberated in the room, and not long after that, Souster looked down at his wristwatch. We knew it was time to go. We never did get Contact Press's side of the story about *I Want to Tell You Love*, and the afternoon calls into question Acorn's misgivings. What we did learn that afternoon was that Souster indeed loved Acorn very much.

As suggested by Acorn's anecdotes, it seems that he had taken charge of finding a home for the book, since the publishers—like Souster—to whom they sent *I Want to Tell You Love* were, mostly, already part of Acorn's literary circle. Beyond *Fiddlehead*, Contact, and M&S, it is not clear if *I Want to Tell You Love* was sent to anyone else for consideration. While Acorn sought publication for the book, bissett was a co-founder of Very Stone House (along with Mayne and Jim Brown) as well as co-founder and publisher of *blewointment*. When I asked bissett why he did not self-publish under either moniker, he replied, "I don't know." And while that answer may be unsatisfying, it is demonstrative of the idiosyncratic nature of self-publishing and small press ventures. Often driven by spontaneity and reflexivity, perhaps it just did not feel right to publish the book in that way.

Three copies of the typescript are known to exist and are all safely stored in valuable archives and special collections in Canada—two at the Clara Thomas Archives at York University and one copy at Library and Archives Canada in Ottawa. The copy of the typescript at the LAC arrived in 1988 and was delivered by William Hoffer Books. bissett has no recollection of how it might have gotten into the famous bookseller's hands, but he speculates that Acorn likely sold Hoffer a copy. The two other nearly identical copies of *I Want to Tell You Love* were donated in 1969 to the York University Library by bissett in a steamer trunk after librarians were persuaded by Birney to "buy Bill's literary hoard" to help raise funds to support him while he was in court on charges for marijuana possession.[81] *I Want to Tell You Love* has safely remained in these holdings ever since.

It seems that Rankin's advice to publish singularly authored collections was apt advice at the time. The sensibility of Canadian readers was still being established by the markets, and a collaborative book of disparate poetic styles would have likely been seen as too much of a risk for a publisher like M&S. Though the collaborative effort of *I Want to Tell You Love* would languish in neglect for decades, many of its poems went on to have vibrant lives on their own. bissett, as more acutely detailed in the "Later Publications and Emendation List" to this edition, published many of his poems in later collections. Poems such as "we sleep inside each other all," "suite of five," "The Body," and "The Fountain" all appeared in his debut collection of poetry *We Sleep Inside Each Other All* (1966), which was published by Nichol. This publication subsequently cemented bissett's reputation as one of Canada's most radical poets on the West Coast at the time and continued to increase the exchange between radical writing communities in Vancouver and Toronto. As for Acorn, many of his poems, too, appeared in later collections. Poems such as "An Afflicted Man's Excuse," "The Damnation Machine," "Detail of a Cityscape," "Poem for a Singer," and "The Schooner" all appeared in *I've Tasted My Blood* (1969). Decades later, in 1983, Acorn would finally publish with M&S. It was a book entitled *Dig Up My Heart, Selected Poems, 1952-83*, which featured some poems that were intended for *I Want to Tell You Love*. Versions of the poems included in *I Want to Tell You Love*, then, are likely familiar to Acorn's and bissett's long time readers; however, it is in their collaborative context—as detailed in the next section—that they begin to perform anew.

Thinking in Mosaics

While the poems of *I Want to Tell You Love* are important works on their own—effectively representing the separate creative orientations of each author—it is within a conversational context that the poems come together in a mosaical presentation. Multiple poetic modes—imagist, concrete, confessional, pastoral, polemical—are advanced by bissett and Acorn like the many pieces of material that comprise a mosaic artwork. When taken individually, these pieces may appear incongruous to the others; however, it is in assemblage that they contribute to a dynamic whole. *I Want to Tell You Love* is a textual example of this kind of creative approach, and it has some affinities with collage and assemblage artistic practices.

As noted in the opening of this introduction, Betts recognizes the congruities between the aesthetic and radical political branches of the avant-garde within the work; he writes, they "recognized a parallel in Acorn's radical politics and bissett's radical formal experiments."[82] Indeed, there are various modes of composition in the typescript, but it is the authors' shared interest in radicalism that provides a rationale for their collaboration. Acorn's radical political verse is distinguished from bissett's radical formal experiments: Acorn often uses poetry to support social and political ideology, and bissett writes with the belief that, along with writing explicitly polemical poems, liberating form possesses the power to change and influence society. Some poets and literary critics such as Al Purdy and Shane Neilson have understated or diminished Acorn's socially inflected poetry that supports radical political ideologies such as Marxism and Communism. However, literary scholar of the Canadian Marxist tradition James Doyle identifies "Acorn's political radicalism as an important element in his life," and this is demonstrated in *I Want to Tell You Love*.[83] On the other hand, bissett's radical formal experiments have been identified as a distinguishing aesthetic feature of his work. bissett is known for his "contempt for the orthodoxies of the printed word"[84] and commitment to "an ever-expansive mode of meaning production,"[85] which is expressed in his inveterate shattering of linguistic conventions such as syntax, grammar, and punctuation. The two positions that Acorn and bissett occupy correspond in a most fundamental sense: radicalism is a devotion to change with a belief in revolutionary possibility. In terms of aesthetics, the poems appear distinct; however, that is the point of their collaboration. According to bissett, they recognized these changes and sought to create from that place:

    a book uv poetree by 2 poets   diffrent n similar
    like gertrude stein sd evreething is a   book uv

> poetree by 2 peopul uv simultaneouslee similar n dissimilar apertures uv consciousness cultural n psychik leenings urges phraseolojees uv lettrs tropes beerings weight uv n breks uv th lines getting 2gethr using conversaysyunal n xplorativ xperimental n mor normativ n poetik fixtures uv langwage arts.[86]

It is in this seeming incongruity that an alternative sociopolitical vision becomes realized.

The alliance of the seemingly discordant voices of bissett and Acorn in mosaic formation makes a significant contribution to the histories of avant-garde literary production because it effectively rediscovers *materialist avant-gardism*—that is, a realization of the oft-theorized alliance of the radical political and aesthetic branches of the avant-garde which Renato Poggioli has identified as distinct and discrete.[87] Expanding upon Poggioli's critique, Matei Călinescu usefully describes materialist avant-gardists— Arthur Rimbaud, for example—as "advanced writers and artists who transferred the spirit of critique of social forms to the domain of artistic forms."[88] These writers and artists sought "to overthrow all the binding formal traditions of art and to enjoy the exhilarating freedom of exploring completely new, previously forbidden, horizons of creativity. For they believed that to revolutionize art was the same as to revolutionize life."[89] bissett's aesthetic experiments and Acorn's political verse are assembled in this spirit.[90]

Materialist avant-gardism is not necessarily an end in itself; radical artistic action requires a program. Explaining the specific sociopolitical impetus that led to this alliance, bissett states that they were writing in response to the "manee taboos against aborsyun gay love sheltrs 4 homeless peopul repressive laws against marijuana whn alcohol was sew encouragd taboos against peopul wanting 2 n protesting against th war in Vietnam politikul writing all these n mor."[91] Indeed, *I Want to Tell You Love* is informed by these turbulent conditions that defined the global social and political landscape, and were deeply felt in Canada. These conditions, too, led to significant divisions among people, at the levels of both citizenship and intergovernmental affairs. These divisions spawned fears of American imperialism, disparagement of Communist ideology, and discrimination against Beatnik artists, which indicate, among many things, a social inclination to see differences before commonality. bissett and Acorn not only express discontent with these conditions in their book, but they also offer a radical response to these problems. Acorn alludes to their intent in his poem "Wouldn't it Be Dreadful" where he writes: "If for our own good they would one day relieve us / of what troubles us . . . Our consciousness?"[92] Here, he suggests that these troubling sociopolitical conditions originate from consciousness—more specifically, as implied by this unlikely collaboration, notions of consciousness that perceive differences between individuals as points of repulsion that actively divide a community.

By assembling the two branches of the avant-garde, Acorn and bissett's seemingly incongruous voices create a hybrid form similar to what French philosopher Roland Barthes proposes in his theories of a Text (as opposed to a work) in 1971 (translated into English in 1979): a pluralistic entity that "cannot be contained by hierarchy" and is a "subversive force in respect of the old classifications."[93] A Text resists notions of conformity and commodity, and most importantly, gestures toward a multiform understanding of consciousness, here called *mosaical consciousness.* This notion emerges from the work of Marshall McLuhan, whose ideas had strong currency in Vancouver during the 1960s. In his examination of Harold Adams Innis, McLuhan abstracts the concept of a mosaic to describe Innis's writing in terms of a "mosaic structure of seemingly unrelated and disproportioned sentences and aphorisms" that work together in "a mutual irritation."[94] Mosaical consciousness demonstrates an intense awareness of one's differences with the external world, but it does not conceive of difference as an impetus for repulsion or a target for standardization. Instead, it is an irritation—that is, a stimulation or active response. Further, mosaical consciousness is a state of awareness resistant to what bissett calls homogenous culture and privileges difference as a stimulus for the mind and community. He writes,

> i gess what we ar all beginning 2 accept n realize is that diffrens is not opposisyun diffrens is enhansing can b   evree brain is diffrent n uv kours that was veree much th   space we wer cumming from ... we wer veree much disappointid n opposd 2 th cultur uv   sameness that was encroaching n trying 2 dominate pepuls lives. [95]

This idea is most effectively communicated by this collaborative text's thematic preoccupation with love—another mode of managing dissimilarity to formulate alliance. It is the "mutual irritation" of bissett's and Acorn's voices that demonstrates this alternative form.

As illustrated by *I Want to Tell You Love*'s history of dismissal, the most striking feature of the typescript is its mosaical presentation: the appearance of disunity in bissett and Acorn's collaboration created by their dissimilar poetic voices. When they began their collaboration, Vancouver's flourishing scene was shared by the established leftists such as Lowther and Livesay as well as the emergent radical poets such as bissett, Copithorne, Gadd, and the TISH poets. While the differing ethos of these groups ensured distinction within certain lines of critical discourse, Vancouver's seemingly divided literary communities were unified by sensitivity to the turbulent sociopolitical conditions of the time. Acorn, having lived in the city for only a short while, recognized this and established numerous forums of political and cultural engagement in an effort to bridge the two communities with his series at the Vanguard Books and the Advance Mattress Coffee House.[96]

I Want to Tell You Love documents the development of bissett's radical aesthetic experiments that readers, editors, and scholars recognize today—notably his unconventional orthography, his destabilization of conventional reading practices (left to right, top to bottom), and his general distrust of language as a means of individual expression. It seems that bissett's aesthetic coalesces just after the completion of *I Want to Tell You Love*. Prior to this moment in 1966, bissett experiments with various modes of writing, which indicates his search for a voice, but also foregrounds the shifting nature of his poetics. In 1962, bissett's first published poems appear in *PRISM* magazine. The poems reflect his endeavour to create a poetic voice. The first poem of this sequence (which is untitled) opens with the lines: "i want to scream out to everyone help me / poet goes to psychiatrist / doubts about his career."[97] This opening presents a facetious image of a poet struggling with his art. Following these lines, however, the speaker's language becomes violent with images such as "pellets of rotten stomach" and "twisted lung" that defamiliarize the body. bissett seeks to destabilize notions of the body and mind as singular and whole entities. This is further suggested in the line "head tooth CRACKD OPEN," which foregrounds his interest in opening up new forms of thinking and speaking. In these poems, bissett stops short of explicitly illustrating the effects of opening the body and mind in this way. However, the poem's frenetic composition and ambition to rethink limits of the body and mind recalls the Surrealist practice of automatic writing—another mode of composition that explores states of consciousness in response to early twentieth-century modernity.

Similar experimentation can be observed in *I Want to Tell You Love* in the poem "when and how over high mountain into high dream out," wherein bissett unfixes the reader's body and mind—the movement of the eyes and cognitive functions—from normative practices of reading and writing. Most of the poem consists of columns of words that can be read vertically and horizontally, shattering semantic direction. The reader, then, is permitted to proceed autonomously, unimpeded by the determinism of conventional left-to-right reading practices. The eyes can move from left to right to create a sequence of words like "know takes returns has" or top to bottom to create "know / next / week / passes / plays / resembles / returns" with many other possible permutations of the reading sequence. As a result, bissett creates an excess of meaning that depends on the individual reader's process of working through the words on the page. In addition, unconventional, yet for bissett signature, spellings emerge in *I Want to Tell You Love* where "you" is contracted to "yu" and "the" becomes "th." Punctuation is avoided, and unstable grammar disrupts any notion of a poem's conventional flow. Both of these poems present experimental methodologies, which ideally destabilize singular notions of the body, text, and authorial voice. These choices become increasingly pronounced as he develops his writing practice.

Further disrupting the coherence of bissett's voice within the typescript and contributing to its mosaical formation, these radical formal experiments emerge alongside some of bissett's more conventional-looking poems such as "The Body"—a free verse poem consisting of standard verse paragraph breaks, left aligned margins, and somewhat standardized punctuation and grammar. "The Body" is remarkably unlike the radical visual experiments that would characterize much of bissett's later writing. Indeed, and considering the alliance of their voices in this collaboration, "The Body" more closely resembles Acorn's verse, but with a greater exploration of abstraction. This modal shift disrupts the consistency of bissett's poetic voice and offers editors an additional rationale for the typescript's rejection. However, "The Body" thematically parallels bissett's previously mentioned experimental compositions that reimagine the body as a heterogeneous and open entity while thinking mosaically about parts and the whole:

> What we had to do
> was to forget in a body since singly we
> each had come to live without hope,
> the belief that all is not repetition
> of the same pain[98]

Verse paragraphs three through seven begin with variations of the phrase "One of THE BODY" which lead into a description of the different roles this body fulfills—in other words, "an artist," "businessman," "leader," and so on. To challenge notions of singularity, bissett plays on the ambiguity of the word "body," which can denote both a singular and plural subject position. The penultimate verse paragraph meditates on the relationship between the two:

> The largeness of THE BODY would increase
> and diffuse hopelessly the initial self-betrayals
> invited aroused to sustain it.
> As a consequence, the belief in self,
> in character would drop away behind
> the larger movement of the General Body.[99]

As if meditating on the consequences of homogenization and singularity, this section of the poem alludes to the loss of a "self" and "character" as "the General Body," a large force that effaces qualities of the self, overtakes "THE BODY,"[100] an idea to which this collaboration generally responds.

In contrast to bissett's disruptive and rapidly shifting aesthetics, Acorn's poetry before 1965 has a singular voice, precision, and stability, as critics such as Purdy and Livesay point out. Acorn's early aesthetic can be grounded in the traditional critical orthodoxies of Imagist modernism.[101] Livesay aligns Acorn with this tradition in her analysis of Acorn's "Charlottetown Harbour," a poem published in *The Brain's the Target* (1960), which she calls "a return to Imagism"[102] and "a still life painting in the Imagist tradition."[103] This concern for the image as the basic unit of construction accurately describes Acorn's aesthetic preoccupation, as evidenced, too, in "AVOID THE BAD MOUNTAIN" where he appeals for more imagistic poetry. Unlike bissett, whose poems are disjunctive and can sprawl across several pages, Acorn's image-based writing strives for poetry characterized by precision and focus. "The Schooner," as it appears in *I Want to Tell You Love*, is composed in free verse, consisting of two stanzas with left-aligned margins and conventional spelling that effectively illustrates Acorn's aesthetic:

> Keen the tools, keen the eyes,
> white the thought of the schooner
> lined on a draughting board,
> fine the stone that ground the fine blind
> and skills, the many fingers
> that stroked and touched it surely
> til, intricate delicate strong,
> it leans poised in the wind.[104]

The language here is economical; he uses few conjunctions and adjectives. The poem is driven by verbs that propel the poem, condensing the construction process of a sail-ready schooner into eight brief lines—from "draughting board" to "the wind." Preceding his collaboration with bissett, Acorn had published four collections, most of which largely employ this singular, consistent, and less overtly political voice. However, in his collaboration with bissett, Acorn does not remain fixed to a single mode of writing. Instead, Acorn shifts into more explicit polemic poems through which he explores his radical socialist politics.

Though there are some exceptions, critical discussion focusing on the radical politics of Acorn's poetry has largely been truncated. Scholars perhaps have been led by Purdy's anecdotal introduction to *I've Tasted My Blood* in which he regrets deviations from Acorn's imagistic signature into a social mode of writing. Purdy writes that Acorn's "Poems written from 1964 to 1968 . . . changed in style and somewhat in content from the earlier poems. . . . In a way I regret these stylistic and thematic differences."[105] This period matches the span of time that Acorn spends in Vancouver. As it has been explored by Doyle, Acorn's more overtly political writing from this period fits within a progressive tradition of mid-twentieth-century writing in Canada. This is literature informed by Marxist and anti-capitalist ideologies that present an alternative to the dominant bourgeois view and frequently express "an enviable faith in the perfectibility of humanity."[106] In the 1950s especially, Acorn's writing—much of which is featured in periodicals—was closely aligned with this tradition, and he looked to liked-minded progressive poets and writers like Joe Wallace and Louise Harvey. Like them, he submitted poems to Communist magazines such as the *Canadian Tribune*, but his poems were distinctive. "Acorn's Communist poetry," Doyle explains, "makes its points by more subtle means, and encompasses a wider variety of form and subject matter"[107] than some of his progressivist peers but is emboldened by similar themes of rebellion, collectivism, idealism, and humanitarian causes. As Doyle points out in *Progressive Heritage*, it is with this kind of writing that Acorn began to develop his skills as a writer in the 1950s and led to early publications such as *In Love and Anger* and *The Brain's the Target*. So, while some of Acorn's friends and critics lament what they see as a departure from his concise imagistic lyrics, his exploration of political content in his poetry is actually a return to it.

In Acorn's numerous contributions to *I Want to Tell You Love*, he attempts to capture and critique the sociopolitical conditions of his time. Some of the poems directly explore themes of anti-capitalism, express worker sympathies, and aspire to human perfectibility, while others border these themes. "One Day Kennedy Died and So Did the Birdman of Alcatraz" references the historically significant deaths of John F. Kennedy and Robert Stroud, and longs for a utopic "heaven of birdsongs"; "The Damnation Machine" describes hell as a place where innocents are unable to defend themselves against an oppressive and ominous force; and "Earnest Word" opens with a quotation from Marxist philosopher Friedrich Engels and questions what it means to be free. These progressive efforts emerge most strongly and compactly in his "Detail of a Cityscape" in which Acorn describes a "cripple" who "struggles/onto the bus" and picks the closest and "most uncomfortable seat; / because if he tried for another / the surge of the bus starting / would upend him."[108] The poem reflects the larger sphere of sociopolitical issues confronted by *I Want to Tell You Love*. Acorn presents a social struggle that occurs within public space: the subject struggles to his designated position on the bus. In response, the poem's diction implores sympathy through words like "aimless," "flopping," and "poor," revealing an agenda that recognizes the subject's tenuous and alienated position, prompting readers to rethink the structure of society and positions of individuals within it. Acorn's movement toward a progressivist mode of writing contrasts his less political imagist lyrics. While the image of the subject is indeed vivid and compact (unlike some of his other political poems), the motivation behind the creation of that image is grounded in a concern for social equality. The juxtaposition of these two modes of writing, imagism—being harder, more precise, and less explicitly political—paired with his polemics, formulates part of the mosaic of poetic styles, just as bissett juxtaposes his own conventional verse against formal experiments. What holds these styles and positions together, for the authors, is love.

Love resonates with the notions of the mosaic explored thus far: a plethora of distinct pieces that, in interplay, formulate a whole. French philosopher Georges Bataille's complex writing on love and eroticism highlights the importance of love for bissett and Acorn's agenda. In *Eroticism*, Bataille sees eroticism and love as disruptive forces, specifically provoking a disruption of the singular notions of individuality; he argues that eroticism enables us to grasp a "conscious refusal to limit ourselves within our individual personalities"[109] and leads "to the blending and fusion of separate objects" which is seen most readily in sex and death; however, we can also see glimpses of these fusions in poetry.[110] The fusing of separate objects has been explored in various historical literary contexts. In Bataille's lifetime, the Surrealists sought to transform notions of an individual's consciousness through the merging of conscious and unconscious minds so that surreality may manifest itself in all aspects of life. However, this agenda to expand consciousness also manifested earlier in the work of the Romantic poets such as William Wordsworth, John Keats, Percy Shelley, and William Blake who, like bissett and Acorn, reacted against tragic social and political conditions of their time.

Accounting for the revolutionary efforts of these Romantic poets, M. H. Abrams traces a preceding reorientation of the individual and their relationship to separate objects with a particular focus on how consciousness can be reinvented by radical notions of love. Abrams argues that "The vision" sought by these poets is "a holy marriage with the external universe, to create . . . a new world which is the equivalent of paradise."[111] In what complements bissett's previously quoted list of taboos and social ills, Abrams suggests that the Romantics reacted against "industrialization, urbanization, and increasingly massive industrial slums; of the first total war and postwar economic collapse; of progressive specialization in work, alterations in economic and political power, and consequent dislocations of class structure; of competing ideologies and ever-imminent social chaos."[112] The realm of Romantic politics is a fruitful context in which to situate bissett's and Acorn's politics, offering a sense of their cosmic idealism, but it also assists in grasping the radical connotations of love as a means of uniting the world and spirit, mind and body that they were working towards. Most importantly, this historical connection draws out the Romantic basis of the avant-garde with which the politics of *I Want to Tell You Love* can be aligned.

Acorn and bissett are regarded as poets with connections to the Romantic spirit. When Purdy notes Acorn's shift toward overtly polemical poetry, he describes these poems as "utopian."[113] Purdy's descriptors characterize Acorn's political poetry in a way that is commensurate with Romantic-era politics, and he admits that Acorn is "somewhat romantic in the best sense."[114] Bowering has also acknowledged the neo-Romantic aspects of Acorn's political poetry; he writes, "His politics are as much a poet's communism as Shelley's were. He's a romantic radical, looking to awaken

Critical Introduction   45

or 'find outside the beauty inside me.' He has the romantic sense of man's perfectibility."[115] Acorn's "Poem for a Singer," which Livesay identifies as an exuberant representation of Acorn's "social revolutionary" spirit, effectively represents this Romantic mode.[116] Livesay notes that the poem is an "affirmation and belief in humanity's struggle . . . in the tradition of Blake and Whitman"[117] and in it sees "the phase of the conscious, social revolutionary poet defying the sickness of capitalist society."[118] Livesay's assessment finely articulates the spirit of the poem including its political goals; however, because she is examining the poem outside of the context of *I Want to Tell You Love*, her analysis can be expanded to address its contribution to the text as a whole. Livesay notes that the poem "ends with his [the speaker's] complete identification of himself with the singer."[119] In "Poem for a Singer," as it appears in *I Want to Tell You Love*, Acorn's speaker not only identifies with the singer, the speaker wants more than that; the speaker cries out, "Let me be the song" and then again, "Oh let me be the / men and women of her song," striving toward empathy for the singer, the workers, the song itself. When expressing his desire to "be" the others, the speaker is expressing a desire to move beyond the restrictions of bodily materiality and to merge with the other beings. In this way, the poem compares with bissett's "The Body," in which he too plays with notions of bodily singularity. Acorn's speaker strives toward a more mosaical form of being, thinking, and seeing: "for the standing up proud and hopeful way, the / way expressing the truth of our lives."[120] "Poem for a Singer" demonstrates the various complex notions of a mosaic as well as the radical social politics that are at the heart of the typescript.

On the other hand, while bissett's writing can be discussed within a discourse of radical aesthetic experimentation, it is useful to note that critics such as Tallman have, as Purdy and Bowering did for Acorn, connected bissett to a Romantic tradition. In his "Statement for bill bissett"—a statement that was written to persuade the Canada Council for the Arts to award bissett funding in 1978—Tallman compares bissett's spirit to that of Shelley. Tallman writes, "I think that Shelley set the standard for a romantic striving after a 'wisdom and spirit of the universe' which, in his own contemporary Canadian way, bissett has so steadfastly sought in his visionary poems."[121] bissett's poem "a carriage that were green" illustrates a neo-Romantic sentiment that reacts (as did Shelley, Wordsworth, and others) against industrialization and crimes against nature. Informed by anti-capitalist and anti-establishment sentiments, the poem criticizes the municipal government, "th mafia boys" as bissett calls them, for tearing down houses in Vancouver—including bisset's own home—and replacing them with shopping complexes; bissett writes,

> o if ever
> there were
> a carriage
> that were
> green,
> mushrooms
> and banners
> flow
> from behind
> stops for
> lunch on
> orange
> toadstools
> blue sky
> above, all
> green
> clear, below.[122]

While this poem is remarkably different from any poem by Shelley—especially in its formal approach—bissett's speaker, in a quintessential Romantic spirit, longs for life in a natural world without industrialization and excessive consumption.

These Romantic associations and their shared revolutionary spirit provide useful entry into the discourse of avant-garde modes of theorization. Călinescu argues that the "concept of avant-garde in radical political thought" emerges in the latter half of the eighteenth century, the beginning of what is generally acknowledged as part of the Romantic period for arts and literature.[123] Călinescu describes the characteristics of a Romantic avant-gardism that includes following an "anti-elitist program" that acknowledges that "life should be radically changed."[124] These attributes most certainly inform *I Want to Tell You Love*'s creation. However, bissett and Acorn's collaboration does not at first glance appear to be a resolutely avant-garde text. Charles Russell describes "the avant-garde writer" as one who "frequently explores limits of the creator's freedom to disrupt syntax and to use new patterns of linguistic association."[125] While some of the disruptive patterns are clearly exhibited in bissett's poems, the collection does not squarely fit Russell's conception. *I Want to Tell You Love*, then, offers an expansion of Russell's definition since it is not purely avant-garde in its syntactic and semantic disruptions, but in its pairing of seemingly incongruous aesthetic approaches that disrupt conventional understanding of the poetry collection as an object created with singular aesthetic and political values. Instead, the book is envisioned as a mosaic. The unusual congruity of bissett and Acorn provides the type of disruption necessary to create a sense of "disorientation," which in turn allows the audience to "experience states of abruptly expanded consciousness,"[126] and it is accepting the implications of this expanded sense of consciousness that could lead to material change.

Acorn and bissett establish the mosaical configuration of their collaboration as a step toward intervening in contemporary sociopolitical affairs—it corresponds with the North American counterculture's search for liberated means of expression and new ways of living with one another. Not only do their poems describe the turbulence of their moment, but they also create art in response to it. The title's singular pronoun "I" acknowledges the collaboration's aspiration to present a mosaic of their voices and indicates their utopian program. In using the singular pronoun (as opposed to the plural "We"), bissett and Acorn depict an idealized vision in which seemingly different individuals conceive of a means of being together without dissolving their singular senses of self. They can see across their differences and find a space to cohabit. They expand the notion of the "I" as a singular letter inhabited by a multitude of forces. The urgency of this vision emerges in the title's unique syntax. bissett and Acorn do not want to passively offer this vision. They do not want to discuss or debate love; they want to achieve the active transference of their vision to the implied reader: to *tell* you love. Instead of writing a collection of poems that presents the vision of their utopia, they create what they believe to be utopia itself: a space in which differences can coexist, a space defined by their idea of love. This vision of love is perhaps a Canadian iteration of the counterculture generation's appeal to love as the antidote to social and political unease.

Avant-gardist programs for social change should always be interrogated when dealing with utopic ambitions. The counterculture, as an attempted cultural revolution, has been interrogated for its failures to achieve its promised revolution—women are still ensnared by repressive gender stereotypes; minority groups, including Black and queer people, still face discrimination and violence; and some aspects of the promised liberated lifestyle have been absorbed by markets and sold back as consumer goods. This is not to say that the legacy of the counterculture was a failure. Indeed, it was significant movement in North America (and elsewhere in the world) which saw a vast number of people believe and act toward new possibilities for being in the world. Utopian cultural movements often have limits—they can risk self-indulgence and exclusion. *I Want to Tell You Love*'s seeming ambition for a utopic vision—along with its invocations of love, co-existence, and social politics—is no different.

Despite his literary fame, Acorn had a notoriously difficult and troublesome personality that caused friction in many of his interpersonal relationships. Some details of Acorn's biography call into question the ways that critics like Jewinski describe "love" for Acorn "as a full, impassioned feeling of fellowhood and brotherhood to man, a love which could repudiate all social rules that infringed upon the dignity of mankind."[127] Regardless of how critics and friends have awkwardly tried to explain away Acorn's troublesome behaviour, his poetic and political philosophy often put him at odds with his community. Acorn's stubborn individualism was an obstacle to his sense of collectivism: "It is a paradox that Acorn has quarrelled violently with every socialist organization he ever had anything to do with, and is a member in good standing of none," writes Purdy.[128] Despite his outward commitments to revolution and social change, Acorn also shied away from the countercultural lifestyle. This is evident first in what Sullivan recognized as his traditional family values and his reluctance to honour his open marriage with MacEwen. Furthermore, in his notes regarding Acorn's time in Vancouver, Jewinski argues that if critics trace the drafts of Acorn's poem "I Shout Love," which appeared in the 1963 *Fiddlehead* special issue, *I've Tasted My Blood*, and the 1972 *I Shout Love and On Shaving Off His Beard*, they can see Acorn attempting "long-winded Charles-Olson-like experiments."[129] He would also "eventually turn away from these experiments in voice and structure" and "often leave this [latter] book off his list of published works."[130] Committed to Canadian nationalist sentiments, Acorn dismissed Vancouver and its countercultural ethos. For him, it was a city which he once saw as a site for potential liberation and instead scorned it as a site of American imperialism.

Unlike Acorn, bissett was unwaveringly committed to the radical lifestyle and aesthetic experiments he began to explore in the 1960s. Following his time with Acorn, bissett continued to embody his anti-establishment politics and embedded himself deeper into Canada's radical literary culture. bissett published dozens of books that were demonstrative of his continually evolving orthography and his innate ability to find new ways of intermixing text, image, and sound. He further explored the possibilities of radical aesthetic experiments and interdisciplinarity through multimedia performances, collaborations with bands like the Mandan Massacre and later The Luddites, and in the visual arts, especially painting, sculpture, and installation. He helped others gain access to a broader audience, like Acorn had helped him, by publishing many new and established poets in his magazine and with his press, including McCaffery, Nichol, Kearns, Gadd, Greg Curnoe, Cathy Ford, Daniel David Moses, and many others. This generosity and commitment to alternative communities, lifestyles, and publishing models did much to establish bissett's reputation. However, while Acorn willfully and intentionally assumed his role as an icon of Canadian literary nationalism, bissett's rise to fame as a now canonized Canadian poet was iconoclastic and largely hinges on his identity as a rebel. bissett, for example, has still not received a Governor General's Award for Poetry. Instead, one of his high honours from the Canadian government came in 1978 when he was condemned by conservative Members of Parliament and accused of publishing pornography, which consequently led to funding cuts for blewointment press.[131] It was a major setback for the press, which bissett eventually sold to David Lee and Maureen Cochrane in 1984 (it became Nightwood Editions). Despite these obstacles, bissett remains active today, painting, writing, and performing, and also working as a member of Secret Handshake, a gallery, clubhouse, and peer support facility for people with schizophrenia in Toronto's Kensington Market.

Based on the pathways that bissett and Acorn followed after 1965, it is clear that they diverged creatively, politically, and physically. bissett maintained a commitment to many of the values he gathered during his countercultural heydays, while Acorn quietly renounced them. With that said, the significance of *I Want to Tell You Love,* should not be discounted. Avant-garde works of literature are not always valuable for their capacity to succeed but are admirable for their attempt to stimulate social change. In striving toward this goal with expansive notions of consciousness, they formulate a mosaical model: Acorn's imagist and political poems and bissett's radical formal experiments march together. Within the context of their poetic mosaic—the "mutual irritation" of their voices—bissett and Acorn formulate a materialist avant-gardism. This mode of avant-garde practice is also attributed to Rimbaud, in whose work "the two avant-gardes, the artistic and the political, tended to merge"[132] and who, in "A Season in Hell" also recognizes that "love must be reinvented."[133] In Rimbaud's thinking, a poet should strive "to reach the unknown, to invent an absolutely new language."[134] In bissett's contributions to the typescript, this attempt to reinvent the semiotic system is certainly present. However, this reinvention is not the central mandate of their collaboration. Instead, they seek to invent an alternative approach to the production of meaning in their disruption of conventional literary practices. *I Want to Tell You Love*, then, offers a means of rethinking our positions in the face of social and political ills. Acorn and bissett offer an example of how discursive differences can correlate and present how they can co-exist within the same space in a way that suggests opposition but is unified by politics, by a desire for love—a salient metaphor to heal a turbulent world.

Afterlives

Acorn left Vancouver and returned east in 1968; bissett remained in the city for many years after that. There is little evidence of much correspondence between the two after the 1960s. It seems that in the final years of his stay in Vancouver, Acorn had even then grown somewhat bitter and disillusioned by the city. In the aforementioned planned book for Very Stone House from 1967, Acorn admits that he and bissett were hardly on speaking terms. He does not allude to whether this was from a conflict or if it was the natural, sometimes inevitable distance that can grow between friends. While the public view of two poets conjoined within a book makes it appear as though they are forever together, this, of course, is not always the case. bissett maintains that he loves Acorn and remembers him fondly.

Acorn had been confident that they would publish *I Want to Tell You Love*. On 16 August 1965, he relays to his mother, Helen: "I've been writing lots of poetry tho I seldom send it out. Somehow I've got to shake myself out of that apathy.... In fact I'm doing something.... I'm bringing out a book called 'I Want to Tell You Love' with a young poet named Bill Bissett."[135] Finally, with decades having passed after Acorn's letter to his mother, *I Want to Tell You Love* is being brought out. And for the first time, this edition offers a glimpse of this peculiar moment in Canadian literary history and the unlikely meeting of two larger than life figures of Canadian letters. Many of the poems, though published separately in later collections, are recast here as poems exploring incongruities and social strife to suggest that difference is important and must be maintained, and further, that generative dialogue can be achieved between persons with seemingly significant differences when love is the animus for the work. Articulating this spirit of their work, bissett claims that "milton n i reelee beleevd that love reseeving it xtending it feeling it was always reelee ther was at th heart uv evreething n we wantid our book 2 show that th brekdown uv sew manee taboos n bcumming kleer 2gethr   all peopul cud subdue th war impulses in our specees."[136]

I Want to Tell You Love identifies a limit of acceptability in publishing in Canada in the mid-1960s. Despite its socially informed congruities, the book was never published. Acorn and bissett eventually abandoned the book and placed those poems in individually authored collections. These poems and their publications led to the productive literary careers of both poets. Had it been published in 1965 as planned, *I Want to Tell You Love* could have served as a beacon of resistance to the culture of sameness that was coming to characterize life in North America. *I Want to Tell You Love* would have been significant to Vancouver's cultural and political climate by offering a clear bridge between its distinctive literary and activist communities and may have inspired additional forms of political and artistic action. In terms of Canada's literary culture, *I Want to Tell You Love* marks a generational transition moment between established and emergent poets, with Acorn representing an old guard and bissett representing an emergent group of radical voices in Canada. Beyond speculation, *I Want to Tell You Love* reminds us of the significant power of literary gatekeepers and their control over the formation of culture in Canada.

NOTES

1. There are currently three typescripts of the book that are known to the editors. The typescripts—typed copies of the poems—are located in two different places: one is currently located in Milton Acorn's fonds at Library and Archives Canada (LAC) in Ottawa and two copies are held in bill bissett's fonds at the Clara Thomas Special Collections at York University in Toronto. These copies are nearly identical in form and content, despite some minor handwritten corrections across the three versions, with some minor variations.
2. J. A. Rankin, 1966 (March 28), Letter to Milton Acorn, Clara Thomas Special Collections, bill bissett fonds, Box 1976 – 002/005, File 14.
3. Milton Acorn, Correspondence with bill bissett, Library and Archives Canada, Milton Acorn Fonds, MG31-D175: Vol. 1, Folder 12.
4. Ed Jewinski, *Milton Acorn and His Works* (Toronto: ECW Press, 1990), 11.
5. Shane Neilson, "Vehement Obfuscation: The Political Poems of Milton Acorn," *Books in Canada*, First published 2003, http://www.booksincanada.com/article_view.asp?id=3547.
6. Steve McCaffery, "Bill Bissett: A Writing Outside of Writing," in *North of Intention: Critical Writings, 1973-1986*, ed. by Karen McCormack (New York: Roof Books, 2000), 93.
7. Ibid, 95.
8. bill bissett. email message to the author, Dec. 30, 2020 and bill bissett, email message to the author, January 2, 2021.
9. Gregory Betts, *Avant-Garde Canadian Literature: The Early Manifestations* (Toronto: University of Toronto Press, 2013), 68.
10. It is difficult to definitively determine if *I Want to Tell You Love* could have been bissett's first book since he could not recall which book had been drafted first. The difference between a publishing timeline and drafting timeline is notable here. It at least seems likely, however, given their temporal proximity, that they were completed around the same time.

11 Ron Dart, "West Coast Literary-Political Clashes: 1960-1985," in *Making Waves: Reading BC and Pacific Northwest Literature*, ed. Trevor Carolan (Vancouver/Abbotsford: Anvil Press – University of Fraser Valley Press, 2010), 150.

12 Dennis Lee, "Cadence, Country, Silence: Writing in Colonial Space," *boundary2* 3, no. 1 (1974): 155.

13 Ibid, 154.

14 Laura Moss and Cynthia Sugars, "Contemporary Period, 1960-1985," in *Canadian Literature in English: Texts and Contexts*, eds. Laura Moss and Cynthia Sugars (Toronto: Pearson Education Canada), 215.

15 Jamie Reid, "The Legacy of Warren Tallman," in *A Temporary Stranger: Homages, Poems, Recollections* (Vancouver: Anvil Press, 2017), 124.

16 Jamie Reid, "th pome wuz a store nd is th storee: th erlee daze uv blewointment," in *A Temporary Stranger*, 77.

17 Canada was complicit with the U. S. Cold War efforts in less direct ways. Canada, for example, supplied American troops with weapons such as napalm and Agent Orange.

18 *Report: Royal Commission on National Development in the Arts, Letters and Sciences, 1949-1951* (Ottawa: Edmond Cloutier, 1951), 17.

19 Ibid, 18.

20 Nick Mount, *Arrival: The Story of CanLit* (Toronto: Anansi, 2017), 5.

21 Pauline Butling, "(Re)Defining Radical Poetics," in *Writing in Our Time: Canada's Radical Poetries in English (1957-2003)* (Waterloo: Wilfrid Laurier Press, 2005), 19.

22 Judith Copithorne, "A Personal and Informal Introduction and Checklist Regarding Some Larger Poetry Enterprises in Vancouver Primarily in the Earlier Part of the 1960s," in *Making Waves: Reading BC and Pacific Northwest Literature*, 92.

23 Irene Niechoda and Tim Hunter, "A Tishstory, edited by Irene Niechoda and Tim Hunter from an afternoon discussion at Simon Fraser University in 1985," in *Beyond Tish*, ed. Douglas Barbour (Edmonton: Newest Press, 1991), 92-3.

24 Warren Tallman, "Wonder Merchants: Modernist Poetry in Vancouver during the 1960's," *boundary2* 3, no. 1 (Autumn 1974), 75.

25 Donald Allen, preface to *The New American Poetry, 1945-1960*, ed. Donald Allen (New York: Grove Press, 1960), xi.

26 Tallman, 67.

27 Milton Acorn, "Avoid Bad Mountain," *Blackfish* no. 3 (1972), n. pag.

28 Jamie Reid, "The Legacy of Warren Tallman," in *A Temporary Stranger*, 132.

29 Ibid, 69.

30 Ibid, 65.
31 Ibid, 67.
32 See Copithorne, "A Personal and Informal Introduction and Checklist."
33 Copithorne, 97.
34 Jamie Reid, "Bob Dylan," in *A Temporary Stranger*, 97.
35 Christine Wiesenthal, *The Half-Lives of Pat Lowther* (Toronto: University of Toronto Press, 2005), 225.
36 See Copithorne, "A Personal and Informal Introduction and Checklist."
37 Michael Turner, "Expanded Literary Practices," in *Ruins in Process*, ed. Lorna Brown. Vancouver Art in the 1960s. The Morris and Helen Belkin Art Gallery & Grunt Gallery. 1 March 2011. http://expandedliterarypractices.vancouverartinthesixties.com/.
38 See Jack Long and Léonard Forest's *In Search of Innocence* (1964), a short documentary for the National Film Board of Canada that focuses on Vancouver's artists, including sculptor Donald Jarvis, painters Jack Shadbolt, Joy Long and Margaret Peterson, and printmaker Sing Lim, but other important figures like bissett, who appears with Lance Farrell, are not credited.
39 Al Purdy, introduction to *I've Tasted My Blood*, by Milton Acorn (Ryerson Press, 1969), viii.
40 Jewinski, 7.
41 Purdy, vi.
42 Rosemary Sullivan, *Shadow Maker: The Life of Gwendolyn MacEwen* (Toronto: Harper Perrenial Canada, 1995), 114.
43 Ibid, 116.
44 Ibid, 130.
45 Ibid, 131.
46 Ibid, 132.
47 Ibid, 132.
48 For more on MacEwen and Acorn's relationship, readers are encouraged to listen to "The Voice Is Intact: Finding Gwendolyn MacEwen in the Archive," a SpokenWeb podcast episode produced by Hannah McGregor.
49 Richard Lemm, *In Love and Anger* (Ottawa: Carleton University Press, 1999), 138.
50 In 1964, Acorn, bissett, Patrick Lane, and the Vancouver literary community suffered the tragic loss of Red Lane.
51 Chris Gudgeon, *Out of this World: The Natural History of Milton Acorn* (Vancouver: Arsenal Pulp Press, 1996), 125.

52 Pierre Coupey, "Straight Beginnings: The Rise and Fall of the Underground Press" in *BC Booklook*, 2012 [Originally published 2007]. https://bcbooklook.com/2012/09/04/other-straight-beginnings-the-rise- and-fall-of-the-underground-press/.

53 Ibid, n. pag.

54 Ibid, n. pag.

55 Acorn, "AVOID BAD MOUNTAIN," n. pag.

56 Ibid, n. pag.

57 Ibid, n. pag.

58 bill bissett, email message to the author, December 31, 2020.

59 bill bissett, "Bill bissett's acceptance speech for Woodcock Award," *BC Booklook*. Last Modified: 2 April 2008, https://bcbooklook.com/2008/04/02/other-bill-bissett-s-acceptance-speech-for-woodcock-award-2/.

60 Tallman suggests that bissett arrived at his signature style in 1966.

61 bill bissett, phone message to the author, January 2, 2020.

62 Gregg Simpson, "Mandan Ghetto." Accessed: 17 August 2020. https://www.greggsimpson.com/ MandanGhetto.htm.

63 Jack Kerouac, "Jack Kerouac, The Art of Fiction No. 41," *The Paris Review* 41, no. 43 (1968). Accessed: 01 May 2018. https://www.theparisreview.org/interviews/4260 /jack-kerouac-the-art-of-fiction-no-41-jack-kerouac.

64 Jamie Reid, "th pome wuz a storee nd is th storee: th erlee daze uv blewointment," in *A Temporary Stranger*, 82.

65 Karl Jirgens, *bill bissett and his Works* (Toronto: ECW Press, 1992), 4.

66 "#105 bill bissett," *B.C. BookLook*. Accessed: 08 May 2018. https://bcbooklook.com /2016/02/02/105-bill-bissett.

67 Jamie Reid, "th pome wuz a storee nd is th storee: th erlee daze uv blewointment," 83.

68 bill bissett, email message to the author, January 2, 2020.

69 bill bissett, interviewed by Eric Schmaltz, "I want to tell you love: Interview with bill bissett," *Open Letter* 15.1 (2012), 58, and pp. 191-92 in this text.

70 Jewinski, 4.

71 Patrick Lane, "bill bissett circa 1967/1968," *The Capilano Review* 2, no. 23 (1997): 87.

72 bissett, *Open Letter*, 59, and pp. 193 in this text.

73 Ibid, 59.

74 Milton Acorn, Correspondence with bill bissett, Library and Archives Canada, Milton Acorn Fonds, MG31-D175: Vol. 1, Folder 12.

75 bissett, *Open Letter*, 58, and pp. 192 in this text.

76 bissett, "Afterword," 189.

77 Milton Acorn, "Note for 'Memoirs of a Total Stranger' By Way of an Introduction," Library and Archives Canada, Seymour Mayne Fonds: Very Stone House Series, MG31-D252: Vol. 14, Folder 5.

78 Ibid, n. pag.

79 Ibid, n. pag.

80 Ibid, n. pag.

81 Earle Birney and Al Purdy, *We Go Far Back in Time: The Letters of Earle Birney and Al Purdy*. Ed. Nicholas Bradley. (Madeira Park, BC: Harbour Publishing, 2014), 182.

82 Betts, *Avant-Garde Canadian Literature: The Early Manifestations*, 68.

83 James Doyle, "'For My Own Damn Satisfaction': The Communist Poetry of Milton Acorn," *Canadian Poetry* 40 (1997), 74.

84 Frank Davey, "Bill Bissett," in *From There to Here: A Guide to English-Canadian Literature Since 1960* (Erin, ON: Press Porcépic), 49.

85 Adeena Karasick, "bill bissett: A WRITING OUSIDE OF WRITING," in *bill bissett: Essays on His Works*, ed. Linda Rogers (Toronto: Guernica Editions, 2002), 50.

86 bissett, *Open Letter*, 59, and pp. 193 in this text.

87 Renato Poggioli, *The Theory of the Avant-Garde*, trans. Gerald Fitzgerald (New York: Icon, 1971), 1-15.

88 Matei Călinescu, *Five Faces of Modernity* (Durham, NC: Duke University Press, 1987), 112.

89 Ibid, 112.

90 Ibid, 112.

91 bissett, *Open Letter*, 61, and pp. 195 in this text.

92 Milton Acorn, "Wouldn't it be dreadful" in *I Want to Tell You Love*, Libraries and Archives Canada. Milton Acorn Fonds, MG31-D175: Vol. 53, Folder 1, n. pag., p. 118 in this text.

93 Roland Barthes, "From Work to Text," in *Image-Text-Music*, trans. Stephen Heath (London: Harper Collins, 1977), 157.

94 Marshall McLuhan, "Media and Cultural Change," in *The Essential McLuhan*, eds. Eric McLuhan and Frank Zingrone (New York: Basic, 1995), 89.

95 bissett, *Open Letter*, 61, and pp. 196-97 in this text.

96 Chris Gudgeon, *Out of this World: The Natural History of Milton Acorn* (Vancouver: Arsenal Pulp Press, 1996), 125.

97   bill bissett, "3 poems," *PRISM* 3, no. 2 (1962): 48.
98   bill bissett, "The Body," in *I Want to Tell You Love*, Libraries and Archives Canada, Milton Acorn Fonds, MG31-D175: Vol. 53, Folder 1, n. pag., p. 93 in this text.
99   Ibid, n. pag., p. 94 in this text.
100 Ibid, n. pag., p. 94 in this text.
101 Louis Dudek usefully describes this mode of writing as "liberation in the direction of contemporary reality, toward the reality of images" and further conceives of "modernism specifically as a line of technical development, in which the image is used as the basic unit in a construction kit" in *The Theory of the Image in Modern Poetry*, 33-35.
102 Dorothy Livesay, "Search for a Style: The Poetry of Milton Acorn," *Canadian Literature* 40 (1969): 33.
103 Ibid, 35.
104 Ibid, 35.
105 Purdy, introduction to *I've Tasted*, xiii.
106 James Doyle, *The Evolution of a Politically Radical Literary Tradition in Canada* (Waterloo, ON: Wilfrid Laurier University Press, 2002), 11.
107 Ibid, 207.
108 Milton Acorn, "Detail of a Cityscape," in *I Want to Tell You Love*, Libraries and Archives Canada, Milton Acorn Fonds, MG31-D175: Vol. 53, Folder 1, n. pag., p. 157 in this text.
109 Georges Bataille, *Eroticism*, trans. Mary Dalwood (London: Penguin, 2012), 24.
110 Ibid, 25.
111 M. H. Abrams, *Natural Supernaturalism: Tradition and Revolution in Romantic Literature* (New York: Norton, 1971), 28.
112 Ibid, 292-93.
113 Purdy, introduction to *I've Tasted*, xiv.
114 Ibid, xii.
115 George Bowering, "Acorn Blood," review of *I've Tasted My Blood* by Milton Acorn, *Canadian Literature* 42 (1969): 85.
116 Dorothy Livesay, "Search for a Style: The Poetry of Milton Acorn," *Canadian Literature* 40 (1969): 40.
117 Ibid, 42.
118 Ibid, 40.
119 Ibid, 41.

120   Milton Acorn, "Poem for a Singer," in *I Want to Tell You Love*, Libraries and Archives Canada, Milton Acorn Fonds, MG31-D175: Vol. 53, Folder 1, n. pag., p. 97 in this text.

121   Warren Tallman, "Statement for bill bissett, September 20, 1978," in *In the Midst: Writings 1962-1992* (Vancouver: Talonbooks, 1992), 99.

122   Warren Tallman, "Statement for bill bissett, September 20, 1978," in *In the Midst: Writings 1962-1992* (Vancouver: Talonbooks, 1992), 99.

123   Călinescu, 101.

124   Ibid, 104.

125   Charles Russell, *Poets, Prophets, and Revolutionaries* (Oxford: Oxford University Press, 1985), 36.

126   Ibid, 35.

127   Jewinski, 11.

128   Purdy, introduction to *I've Tasted*, x.

129   Jewinski, 32.

130   Ibid, 33.

131   See Ryan J. Cox. "HP Sauce and the Hate Literature of Pop Art: bill bissett in the House of Commons." *English Studies in Canada*, 37, nos. 3-4 (2011): 147–62, and Don Precosky. "bill bissett: Controversies and Definitions." *Canadian Poetry* 27 (Fall/Winter 1990). Accessed: 01 May 2018. http://canadianpoetry.org/volumes/vol27/precosky.html.

132   Matei Călinescu, *Five Faces of Modernity* (Durham, NC: Duke University Press, 1987), 113.

133   Arthur Rimbaud, *Collected Poems: Arthur Rimbaud*, trans. Martin Sorrel (Oxford: Oxford University Press, 2011), 222.

134   Quoted in Călinescu, 112.

135   Quoted in Lemm, *Milton Acorn: In Love and Anger*, 142.

136   bissett, *Open Letter,* 61, and pp. 194 of this text.

BIBLIOGRAPHY

"#105 bill bissett." *B.C. BookLook.* Accessed: 08 May 2018. https://bcbooklook.com/2016/02/02/105-bill-bissett.

Abrams, M. H. *Natural Supernaturalism: Tradition and Revolution in Romantic Literature.* New York: Norton, 1971.

Acorn, Milton. *Against a league of liars.* Toronto: Hawkshead Press, 1960.

———. "Avoid Bad Mountain." *Blackfish* no. 3 (1972): n. pag.

———. *The Brain's the Target.* Toronto: Ryerson Press, 1960.

———. Correspondence with bill bissett. Library and Archives Canada. Milton Acorn Fonds. MG31-D175: Vol. 1, Folder 12.

———. *Dig Up my Heart: Selected Poems 1952-83.* Toronto: McClelland and Stewart, 1983.

———. *Hundred proof earth.* Toronto: Aya Press, 1988.

———. "The Idea of a Poem: An Interview with Milton Acorn." Interview by John Pearce. *Canadian Poetry: Studies, Documents, Reviews* 21 (1987): 93-102.

———. *In a Springtime Instant: Selected Poems.* Edited by James Deahl. Oakville: Mosaic, 2012.

———. *I shout love and other poems.* Toronto: Aya Press, 1987.

———. *The Island Means Minago.* Toronto: NC Press, 1975.

———. *I've Tasted My Blood.* Toronto: Ryerson Press, 1969.

———. *Jackpine sonnets.* Toronto: Steel Rail Educational Pub., 1977.

———. *Jawbreakers.* Toronto: Contact Press, 1963.

———. *More Poems for People.* Toronto: NC Press, 1972.

———. *The Northern Red Oak: Poems for and about Milton Acorn.* Toronto: Unfinished Monument Press, c1987.

———. "Note for 'Memoirs of a Total Stranger' By Way of an Introduction." Library and Archives Canada. Seymour Mayne Fonds: Very Stone House Series. MG31-D252: Vol. 14, Folder 5.

———. "Poem for a Singer." *The Literary Review* 8, no. 4 (1965): 511-13.

———. *A Stand of Jackpine: Two Dozen Canadian Sonnets.* Toronto: Unfinished Monument Press, 1987.

———. *To Hear the Faint Bells.* Hamilton: Hamilton Haiku Press, 1996.

———. *The Uncollected Acorn.* Toronto: Deneau, 1987.

———. *Whiskey Jack.* Toronto: HMS Press, 1986.

Acorn, Milton, and bill bissett. *I Want to Tell You Love*. Libraries and Archives Canada. Milton Acorn Fonds. MG31-D175: Vol. 53, Folder 1.

Allen, Donald, ed. *The New American Poetry, 1945-1960*. New York: Grove Press, 1960.

Atwood, Margaret. *Survival: A Thematic Guide to Canadian Literature*. Toronto: Anansi, 1972.

Barbour, Douglas, ed. *Beyond Tish*. Edmonton: Newest Press, 1991.

Barthes, Roland. *Image-Text-Music*. Translated by Stephen Heath. London: Harper Collins, 1977.

Bataille, Georges. *Eroticism*. Translated by Mary Dalwood. London: Penguin, 2012.

Betts, Gregory. *Avant-Garde Canadian Literature: The Early Manifestations*. Toronto: University of Toronto Press, 2013.

Birney, Earle, and Al Purdy. *We Go Far Back in Time: The Letters of Earle Birney and Al Purdy*. Ed. Nicholas Bradley. Madeira Park, BC: Harbour Publishing, 2014.

bissett, bill. "3 poems." PRISM 3, no. 2 (1962): 48-9.

———. *Awake in the red desert: a recorded book*. Vancouver: Talonbooks & see/Hear Productions, 1968.

———. *Beyond Even Faithful Legends / Selected Poems*. Edited by bill bissett. Vancouver: Talonbooks, 1980.

———. email message to the author, December 31, 2020.

———. email message to the author, January 2, 2021.

———. *fires in th tempul OR Th jinx ship nd othr trips: pomes-drawings-collage*. Vancouver: Very Stone House, 1966.

———. *Heat makes th heart's window for Martina*. Toronto: Coach House Press, 1967.

———. "I want to tell you love: Interview with bill bissett." By Eric Schmaltz. *Open Letter* 15, no. 1 (2012): 58-63.

———. *NOBODY OWNS TH EARTH*. Toronto: Anansi, 1971.

———. *Of th land divine service: poems*. Toronto: Weed/flower Press, 1968.

———. phone message to the author, January 2, 2020.

———. *Stardust*. Vancouver: Blewointment press, 1975.

———. *Sunday work: A marvellous experience*. Vancouver: Blewointment Press, 1969.

———. *We sleep inside each other all : poems, prose & drawings*. Toronto: Ganglia, 1966.

———. *What fuckan theory; a study of language*. Toronto: Ganglia Press, 1972.

———. *Where is Miss Florence Riddle?* Toronto: Fleye Press, 1967.

bissett, bill, ed. *blewointment magazine* 1, nos.1-2 (1963).

———. *blewointment magazine* 2, nos. 2-4 (1964).

———. *blewointment magazine* 3, no. 1 (1965).

———. *blewointment magazine* 4, no. 1 (1966).

———. *blewointment magazine* 5, nos. 1-2 (1967-1968).

———. *The Combined Blewointment Picture Book nd the News*. Vancouver: Blewointment Press, 1972.

———. *Facist Court*. Vancouver: Blewointment Press, 1970.

———. *occupation issew*. Vancouver: Blewointment Press, 1970.

———. *Oil slick speshul*. Vancouver: Blewointment Press, 1971.

———. *Poverty isshew*. Vancouver: Blewointment Press, 1972.

———. *What Isint Tantrik Speshul*. Vancouver: Blewointment Press, 1973.

Bowering, George. "Acorn Blood." Review of *I've Tasted My Blood*, by Milton Acorn, *Canadian Literature* 42 (1969): 84-86.

Butling, Pauline, and Susan Rudy. *Writing in Our Time: Canada's Radical Poetries in English (1957-2003)*. Waterloo: Wilfrid Laurier Press, 2005.

Călinescu, Matei. *Five Faces of Modernity*. Durham: Duke University Press, 1987.

Canada. *House of Commons Debates*. 2 December 1977. (Bob Wenman, PCPC). https://parl.canadiana.ca/view/oop.debates_HOC3003_02/383?r=0&s=3.

———. *House of Commons Debates*. 13 December 1977. (Bob Wenman, PCPC). https://parl.canadiana.ca/view/oop.debates_HOC3003_02/741?r=0&s=3.

———. *House of Commons Debates*. 3 April 1978. (Hugh A. Anderson, LPC). https://parl.canadiana.ca/view/oop.debates_HOC3003_04/710?r=0&s=3.

———. *House of Commons Debates*. 27 June 1978. (Bob Wenman, PCPC). https://parl.canadiana.ca/view/oop.debates_HOC3003_06/955?r=0&s=3.

Copithorne, Judith. "A Personal and Informal Introduction and Checklist Regarding Some Larger Poetry Enterprises in Vancouver Primarily in the Earlier Part of the 1960s." In *Making Waves: Reading BC and Pacific Northwest Literature*, edited by Trevor Carolan, 89-101. Vancouver/Abbotsford: Anvil Press – University of Fraser Valley Press, 2010.

Coupey, Pierre. "Straight Beginnings: The Rise and Fall of the Underground Press." *BC Booklook*, 2012 [Originally published 2007]. https://

bcbooklook.com/2012/09/04/other-straight-beginnings-the-rise-and-fall-of-the-underground-press/.

Cox, Ryan J. "HP Sauce and the Hate Literature of Pop Art: bill bissett in the House of Commons." *English Studies in Canada*, 37, nos. 3-4 (2011): 147–62.

Dart, Ron. "West Coast Literary-Political Clashes: 1960-1985." In *Making Waves: Reading BC and Pacific Northwest Literature*, edited by Trevor Carolan, 143-60. Vancouver/Abbotsford: Anvil Press – University of Fraser Valley Press, 2010.

Davey, Frank. "Bill Bissett." In *From There to Here: A Guide to English-Canadian Literature Since 1960*, 49-54. Erin, ON: Press Porcépic.

Deahl, James. "Acorn and the Revolutionary Mind." *Cross-Canada Writers' Quarterly* 8, nos. 3/4 (1986): 13-58.

Doyle, James. "'For My Own Damn Satisfaction': The Communist Poetry of Milton Acorn." *Canadian Poetry* 40 (1997): 74-87.

———. *Progressive Heritage: The Evolution of a Politically Radical Literary Tradition in Canada*. Waterloo, ON: Wilfrid Laurier University Press, 2002.

Dudek, Louis. *The Theory of the Image in Modern Poetry*. St. John's: Pratt Lecture, 1979.

Embra, Maurice, dir. *Strange Grey Day This*. Vancouver: Canadian Broadcasting Corporation, 1965.

Fetherling, George. *Travels by Night: A Memoir of the Sixties*. Toronto: Lester Publishing, 1994.

Forest, Léonard, dir. *In Search of Innocence*. Toronto: National Film Board of Canada, 1964.

Frye, Northrop. "Conclusion to *A Literary History in Canada*." In *The Bush Garden: Essays on the Canadian Imagination*, 213-51. Toronto: Anansi, 1971.

Gudgeon, Chris. *Out of this World: The Natural History of Milton Acorn*. Vancouver: Arsenal, 1996.

Jewinski, Ed. *Milton Acorn and His Works*. Toronto: ECW Press, 1990.

Jirgens, Karl. *bill bissett and His Works*. Toronto: ECW Press, 1992.

Karasick, Adeena. "bill bissett: A WRITING OUSIDE OF WRITING." In *bill bissett: Essays on His Works*, edited by Linda Rogers, 50-71. Toronto: Guernica Editions, 2002.

Kerouac, Jack. "Jack Kerouac, The Art of Fiction No. 41." *The Paris Review* 41, no. 43 (1968). Accessed: 17 March 2021. https://www.theparisreview.org/interviews/4260/the-art-of-fiction-no-41-jack-kerouac.

Lane, Patrick. "bill bissett circa 1967/1968." *The Capilano Review* 2, no. 23 (1997): 85-8.

Lee, Dennis. "Cadence, Country, Silence: Writing in Colonial Space." *boundary2* 3, no. 1 (1974): 151-68.

———. *Civil Elegies and Other Poems*. Toronto: Anansi, 1972.

Lemm, Richard. *Milton Acorn: In Love and Anger*. Ottawa: Carleton University Press, 1999.

Livesay, Dorothy. "Search for a Style: The Poetry of Milton Acorn." *Canadian Literature* 40 (1969): 33-42.

McGregor, Hannah. "The Voice Is Intact: Finding Gwendolyn MacEwen in the Archive." 6 April 2020, in *SpokenWeb Podcast*, produced by SpokenWeb, MP3 Audio, https://spoken web.ca/podcast/episodes/the-voice-is-intact-finding-gwendolyn-macewen-in-the-archive/.

McCaffery, Steve. "bill bissett: A Writing Outside of Writing." In *North of Intention: Critical Writings, 1973-1986*, edited by Karen MacCormack, 93-106. New York: Roof, 2000.

McLuhan, Marshall. "Media and Cultural Change." In *The Essential McLuhan*, edited by Eric McLuhan and Frank Zingrone, 89-96. New York: Basic, 1995.

Moss, Laura, and Cynthia Sugars. "Contemporary Period, 1960-1985." In *Canadian Literature in English: Texts and Contexts*, edited by Laura Moss and Cynthia Sugars, 215. Toronto: Pearson Education Canada, 2009.

Mount, Nick. *Arrival: The Story of Can Lit*. Toronto: Anansi, 2017.

Neilson, Shane. "Vehement Obfuscation: The Political Poems of Milton Acorn." *Books in Canada*, 2003. http://www.booksincanada.com/article_view.asp?id=3547.

Niechoda, Irene, and Tim Hunter. "A Tishstory, edited by Irene Niechoda and Tim Hunter from an afternoon discussion at Simon Fraser University in 1985." In *Beyond Tish*, edited by Douglas Barbour, 92-3. Edmonton: Newest Press, 1991.

Poggioli, Renato. *The Theory of the Avant-Garde*. Translated by Gerald Fitzgerald. New York: Icon, 1971.

Precosky, Don. "bill bissett: Controversies and Definitions." *Canadian Poetry* 27 (Fall/Winter 1990). Accessed: 01 May 2018. http://canadianpoetry.org/volumes/vol27/precosky.html.

Purdy, Al. Introduction to *I've Tasted My Blood*, by Milton Acorn, vii-xv. Toronto: Ryerson Press, 1969.

Rankin, J. A. 1966 (March 28). Letter to Milton Acorn. Clara Thomas Special Collections. bill bissett fonds. Box 1976-002/005, File 140.

Reid, Jamie. *A Temporary Stranger: Homages, Poems, Recollections.* Vancouver: Anvil Press, 2017.

Report: Royal Commission on National Development in the Arts, Letters and Sciences, 1949-1951. Ottawa: Edmond Cloutier, 1951.

Rimbaud, Arthur. "A Season in Hell." In *Collected Poems: Arthur Rimbaud*, translated by Martin Sorrel, 210-59. Oxford: Oxford UP, 2011.

Russell, Charles. "The Theory of the Avant-Garde." In *Poets, Prophets, and Revolutionaries*, 3-38. Oxford: Oxford University Press, 1985.

Schmaltz, Eric. "'to forget in a body': Mosaical Consciousness and Materialist Avant-Gardism in bill bissett and Milton Acorn's Unpublished *I Want to Tell You Love*," *Canadian Literature* 222 (Autumn 2014): 96-112.

Simpson, Gregg. "Mandan Ghetto." Accessed: 17 August 2020. https://www.greggsimpson.com/MandanGhetto.htm.

Sullivan, Rosemary. *Shadow Maker: The Life of Gwendolyn MacEwen.* Toronto: Harper Perennial Canada, 1995.

Tallman, Warren. "Statement for bill bissett, September 20, 1978." In *In the Midst: Writings 1962-1992*, 95-102. Vancouver: Talonbooks, 1992.

———. "Wonder Merchants: Modernist Poetry in Vancouver during the 1960s" *boundary*2 3, no. 1 (1974): 57-90.

Turner, Michael. "Expanded Literary Practices." In *Vancouver Art in the 1960s. Ruins in Process*, The Morris and Helen Belkin Art Gallery & Grunt Gallery. Accessed: 1 Mar. 2011. http://expandedliterarypractices.vancouverartinthesixties.com/.

Wiesenthal, Christine. *The Half-Lives of Pat Lowther.* Toronto: University of Toronto Press, 2005.

I Want to Tell You Love

Milton Acorn and bill bissett

Untitled by Milton Acorn

Lover that I hope you are ... Do you need me?
For the vessel I am is like of a rare crystal
that must be full to will any giving. Only
such a choice at the same time is acceptance,
as it is a demand high and arrogant.

Christ! I talk about love like a manoeuver of
armored knights, with drums and banners!
Is it for you whose least whisper against my skin
can twang me like a guitar-string? for
myself? or for something stronger than the saw
that cuts diamonds, yet is only a thought of perfection?

And this is not guarantee, only a promise
made by one who can't judge either his weakness
or his strength ... but must throw them
like dice, one who never intended to play
for small stakes, but once having made the second greatest gamble
and lost, lives for the next total throw.

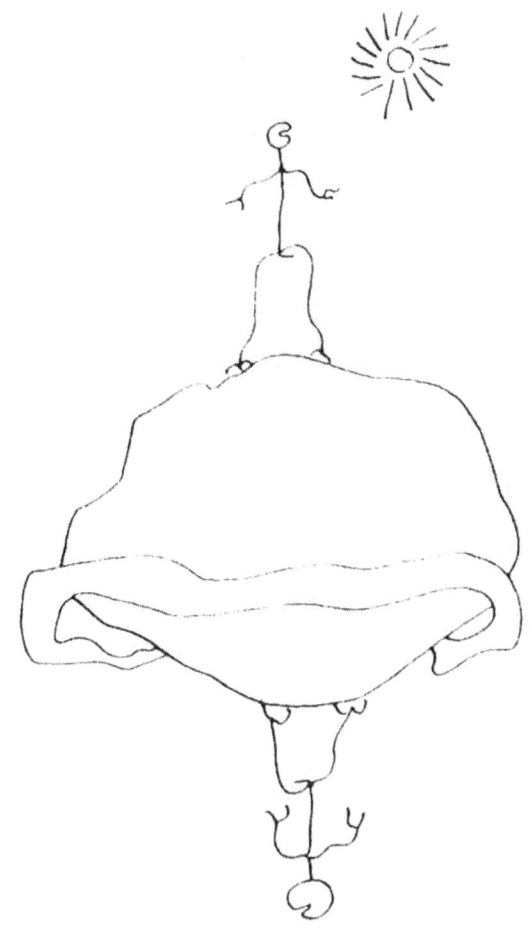

Crossing Directions by bill bissett

1.

Of the universe, one spirit
should be held up, to the many
stars we know shine within
ourselves.

       One love can be known
all loves pay homage to.

The rose, the sea, white or deep,
the colors are many and one
in resolve; the fire, demons, past
for an angel, all human
in spirit. You can speak beauty
of any flower.

       Young girls, rose
again, and boys play summer evening
games outside. And they are inside, the
walls are that artificial, useful
to believe in.

2.

Sometimes I have been afraid
that Time consumes us, afraid as
the Metaphysical poets were, Marvell,
the game of the chariot, as others are,
that we burn ahead of the game.

This summer evening, our daughter
asleep within her precious golden
hope, she let me know we are
always in Time, in time; the cow
on her story-book in the pasture, she sd
"he's not in his house; O, there he goes
into his house." She also sd,
"we fly high to fall, we
have to be broken to die."

3.

The tempo, our eyelids,
open, shut, open in tune
with our bodies warmth,
how we see what is
in front of ourselves, and
behind, our spirit is
always.

We wear color
to the bone.

Sit an evening alone. Write
a poem in favor of
what you see, how many
are the flavors
of your only vision.

Memory is
everywhere.

4.

this time, that one, when,
tomorrow, always living,
pilgrims, saints, ghouls, and evil
is for our creation at will;
these are my suppositions.

as theology will have it, the
darker the green in shadow, more
intense is the discernd light.

and only the moon knows
how revolutions grow, turning,
over and over, always into shore
as the sea's response.

you follow paths; they lead
onto other paths, more meetings,
they hook onto ladders, they
shoot stars, they are ourselves.

5.

the stone, the rock, the boulder,
the lion at the mountain's edge;
light guides; darkness hides.
only hidden is desire for light
in darkness all light resides.

tonight, writing this poem, in no
company other than my self's life,
my woman's; tomorrow, the
meaning of this poem unfolds.

In the desert the hills appear
closer than they are; you climb
for so long to sit on the ridge,
looking down at the salt flats.

The grill-work on the balcony
here, in Vancouver, is like the same
in Mexico. All art is present
in all time, the metaphor
being love.

6.

faces of snow children in
the window, sing carols at Christmas,
bells, frost-bite, candy, promises, how
the music soars, the faith even so little,
as I remember it, to forget what faith
is lacking; the lamp, stored away
in the trunk for four months, shines
brightly, I return from the sea
to see that swell again in her hair.

The butterfly is the wing
of the sun
that makes water,
is the spirit soaring
through the rose.

Magic is
everywhere.

poet and woman

bissett/63

Milton Acorn and bill bissett

An Afflicted Man's Excuse by Milton Acorn

If all lights fell on me differently,
if the music differed, and the voices
were others, perhaps I'd know better
who I am: but now I can only guess it

thru my refusals (like some one kind of person
, wonderful maybe, at least strange,
were going thru something like an orchard,
picking and throwing down). So many things

of which I say "Yes ... I admire that!"
but what is it keeps me from folding
the whole damn basketball of stars
into my bosom? Why can't I give

my most personal love, which I've often said
was universal, whenever it's asked? You need
such a precise almighty balance with me
as to what you come on with, and what you hold back.

Poem by Milton Acorn

Hair flowing yellow and still
to her shoulders, I
saw my sister once
stand before a new flower
and in a hushed voice
give it a name:

and as she cupped
her first gardenia
under her collar bone
today I held
as a vein round my heart
an unwritten poem;

a word --- a few words
delicate as linked blossoms,
more delicate
being thoughts, and
only when winds start
licking them to nothing

do I write so
I may bring you my poem
to find the music of a name,
its vowel-tones to my ears
as a flower reflected in her eyes.

The Slaughter of Innocents by Milton Acorn

The high king's white horse steps mightily
but with dignity, ponderous grace to the fetlock,
dainty descent of the heavy hoof. His rider sits straight
against absurdity, and pouts his rage.

Blown blood flecks the pure hair
of that hoof, and the animal snorts his beauty.
No scream of incomprehensibly realized pain
'll escape him this time. Among killed babies
and mothers wrenched out of the crooning time into agony
he knows only the excitement of scent.

After the orgy of murder the orgy of rape.
The soldier stinks and hisses, "Here
's another for your womb!" The king sits tall
and affects a contemptuous dignity, even feels it.
Now and then he jerks the reins ... the toss
of that maned neck has the distance of thunder.

Untitled by bill bissett

asleep on time
my clothes are shadows of animals
          gathered in my room
tomorrow they invade the city
       to crown the unicorn

toy town: i say 2 yew
          you have channeld everything
          into a continuum
              of precise and strategic
          references

The Schooner by Milton Acorn

Keen the tools, keen the eyes,
white the thought of the schooner
lined on a draughting board,
fine the stone that ground the fine blade
and skills, the many fingers
that stroked and touched it surely
til, intricate delicate strong,
it leans poised in the wind.

The wind that has its own ways,
pushing eddying rippling invisible
in light or darkness;
now no engineer or engine
can guide you but
only the delicacy of touch against touch
underneath the breathing heaven.

Spartacus by Milton Acorn

Never to forgive
a hand with blood
in its fissures,
not to acknowledge it
his property, but
to peer out
thru the stain creeping
between his mindseye
and the world crying
"Look!"

Sparrows peck wings
out of dust, men
create their souls
out of defiance. Not
to acknowledge,
never to forgive
the curses, the commands
to be something less
than the choice of joy.

a carriage
that were
green by bill bissett

th mafia boys
check out
th houses
on our street
to decide

among them
selves ones
they will
tear down
first

o, if ever
there were
a carriage
that were
green,

mushrooms
and banners
flow
from behind

stops for
lunch on
orange
toadstools

blue sky
above, all
green
clear, below

sun turns
carriage
wheels

clouds, exhaust
of dragon snouts

over
pyramid
lake,

how th sun
cums up, what
music
provides
accompaniment

thunderbolt,
streamers
and, for this is
all literal, the
chorus of angels

th palpable
sun rays thru
moss on rock,

two months
to find
another
place, the
shopping complex
will be big

my hands
bounce off
rays, remember
a tall iris,
all that true

and demands
our evacuation

two months
is plenty
of time

for all that,
th mafia
has glamor

Self-Portrait by Milton Acorn

I've got quite a face, thank God,
for smiling or scowling;
tho the smile doesn't earn me much
(so knowingly innocent

and forgiving of all
they bewilderingly find themselves to be
people wonder what they've done
and edge away from me)

: but the scowl --- that's useful!
especially when I stick a cigar in it
... if they've got any plans
for bringing me crashing down on it

they give them up. In either case
no one believes in the puddle of mother's milk
that almost floats my heart, or how
the miracle of a human being's existence

disarms me. I guess I see enough evil
as it is, without it being tossed like acid
in my eyes
--- the way most people get it.

Untitled by Milton Acorn

My poor friends. You aren't beautiful
... the truest touch, the touch of souls
, is painful; but
I see dancers on your shoulders.

Dancers? I said? Is it a title
for one as flamey grave as these?
They bow at me from their heights, their very
beards wave like clustered lions' tails

but their eyes are muffles of clouds, and
for voices I must listen to something innerly deep
going boom ... boom ... boom like surf on a beach
where the rocks are all hearts and shudder but stand strong.

from five poems for norman mailer by bill bissett

1.

as God blew bubbuls

there were six
people
on th moon

one drank sawdust
one prayd
one laughed

one loved
one ate
the others

while i slept

in a jasmine bowl
floating on th waters

a vessel
to carry
us all

down
to earth

Perfect by Milton Acorn

Moments of inlet vision, moments
when the ugly world strikes
like a swung door.
All of a sudden ...

Perfect! I blew
a smoke-ring! Never can do
when I try it; but
as for my life it seems a
succession of efforts
... gestures really

: then in the act of what's loosely called
'loving' a wave (I swear
all the cells jerk)
washes clean thru me:

or I bang my fingertip
down on the page,
"That's IT!" and take off
on rockets
in all directions

. Later I wonder
"What did it?" Is it the coming
together of me an a symbol
that momentarily becomes
me? a crossing of two
lines always changing
in time? or

a slit of light,
blinding, sudden, and
just for an instant,
in the black bag
of another's existence

(her reflexes, her
expediencies, her fumbling
love and approximations of living,
even her lies
held with a desperation
maybe forgotten)?

Whatever it is it lasts ... for
ever and ever
I'm a boy on a swing,
winds reversing always
over the night-sky my carpet.

Poem for Sydney by Milton Acorn

Wisdom makes us hesitant
... true, but
it's no wisdom that doesn't sometimes
make us bold

; or wish to be bold. No one wise
as I hope
      I am
          could look
into the dewy country of
your smile
and not think of loving.

There are few things left for
a heart echoing like mine is
... the horses are gone
    , the sparrows
are rare: in this far land the robins
sound embarrassed

          ...
  but I love the way you sing,
  almost whispering, as if you thought aloud
among the ridges
         of each man's or woman's
ear.

The Body by bill bissett

we are haunted no longer by beauties
not our own though we still entertain
visions of ourselves as lone survivors

So we rode far out to the strawberry island,
sleeping with the scents of marshmallow
and mushroom, stung by salt-spray,
fierce white of what we had stifled
in ourselves to do this. What we had to do
was to forget in a body since singly we
each had come to live without hope,
the belief that all is not repetition
of the same pain

            One of THE BODY was to
be artist to steal the dreams of each of
the rest to make his to make believe
that only he dreamt

            One of THE BODY was to
be businessman to charge money that
we could see and make dirty for transaction
of dreams and that we could say is only
the businessman's dirt.

            One of THE BODY was to
be leader, that only he for us could
correctly interpret the best dreams, but
that all dreams had come from all
and each of us equally, while another
was to be priest, to say that the best

dream was not really ours, but another's
one that could not be seen, not the body's.

           A stream of THE BODY was
to be family, that the self-betrayal of each
of its members might be absorbed in
a general rancour.

           These many ones of THE BODY
overlay nothing that we had not stifled
in ourselves, that we would and could
not find out of what we had done to
ourselves. The mushroom of the journey
to be held high by one of our journey,
the medicine-man, not the priest, did not
either overlay anything in ourselves that
we had stifled to forget as a Body.
The mushroom would always be
itself, an antithesis to what we have
tried to do as a Body, most only when
it was, neither before or after, as causality.

           The dolls of our children,
their frustrated own images motion of shock
against knowledge and time, there would
be nothing to do au naturel as a Body
The largeness of THE BODY would increase
and diffuse hopelessly the initial self-
betrayals invited aroused to sustain it.
As a consequence, the belief in self,
in character would drop away behind
the larger movement of the General Body.

We took in spices to make THE BODY
palatable, and what we could. What some
of us, stranded on a problem plateau
of the magic mountain, the strawberry
island, have had to do is to attempt our retreat from
the General Body, to let it go on without
us, to no longer allow truth to include
ourselves. Doing this we have found
is still to live without hope. Our sense
of hope has been permanently altered or
damaged through our involvements with
THE BODY. We are not the same as we
were inside THE BODY, or as we were
coming to it or taking our departure.
We have become outside remembrance
and forgettings, its illusions and skills,
outside time.

Poem for a Singer by Milton Acorn

Let me be the mane that swings
(clouds tossing, lightning-shot)
about the singer's muscled face,
caressing and letting it go wild.

Or let me be the oars' pulse
throbbing thru that figurehead
to the heroic Argo, that woman alive
who sang against the crash of spray

over her nipples, her chin,
and every love-wrought pore of her,
against the flattening calm, visions
washing up and down her spine.

I've tried to get that touch,
sufficient enough in myself to know
what's loved must fly its own directions
for sake of all my fantasies.

She sings, and it seems to be my lips
which curl about a prisoner's curse,
I who watch while graves pop open
and the dead sing of how they've lived.

She sings in a crowded coffee shop,
smoke curling among tenuous ghosts
of the living : "Love!" she cries.
They scratch at love with palsied hands.

A pale assemblage of moons with no planet,
their mouths pluck as easily into a sneer
as to a yawn: "Sorrow!" cries the singer
... but their diluted tears ...

"Courage!" cries the singer; but today
only the stupid or the very wise are brave.
"Justice!" Right now they won't be just
even to themselves, even to their souls

squirming like worms on a hook. No gods
they have but grey abstractions mulling
in the flaccid null-brain of Moloch: and
they live not by their own hopes but by his.

She sings as time and place have fated her
to people teetering on the last rung
of the last ladder down to the abyss;
who, one foot wavering down, feeling nothing

... feeling nothing but death for themselves,
desire the death of the entire world, because
even the imagination of life
is forbidden by all their teachers.

Let me be the song! Take me
as part of your beauty or an insult, like
a firebird above the last cloud of the last
dark planet, whose song of colored light

speeds into emptiness, creates emptiness,
transmogrifies emptiness to something like
itself, its sweet self. Oh let me be
that singer herself, with her guitar

crossed like a shield over her heart,
perched on this bomb of a world, every instant
ticking .. ticking ... Remembering,
remembering that she lives. Oh let me be

like the men and women of her song, those workers
who living in the very air made hideous
by the oppressor's breath, fought him
for every loose atom of their humanity. Oh let me be

in these that might be the world's last days
be brave as they were, as the singer is ... This heart
is necessary; even in the shadow
of Mount Death, it's necessary

: for the standing up proud and hopeful way, the
way expressing the truth of our lives,
we ought to die
is the only way we might live.

Adam and Eve as Dancers by Milton Acorn

Tongues, sinuous as lightning, issuing
from the mouths of the blessed beyond all legends
--- strong they are and red bright as voices ---
presenting to each foot's gesture its supple place.

I'm thinking of two dancers, Adam and Eve
shining in the bird belled garden ... her hair's a sway
wild orange about her and caught up at the waist;
and the serpent he's the beauty of far sung places,
while the tree nods its apples --- bites of a melody

that sings them. All the distances of lives
from time's end to time's end, are lost and the moments found
... the moments chuckled inward to the spot of souls,
where colored light is all the world, and

the dancer's sway: Adam's foot curves
and sets itself in the place, precisely that place
which this second of joy has chosen ... the rosey head
of his penis slaps the vessel of all the delights to come.

Oh yes are all the babes grown tall. They shall be proud
as their happiest shout, as the tip-top leaf
skimming the honey off heaven, tossing it down
to thrill the dancers' lips, and even this sorrowing minute
I am shall be returned to and blessed in the long dance.

there is the voodoo in the town by bill bissett

there is the voodoo in the town

              drink it down
  period

law and order a family job halifax three members of a halifax family
are doing their part for law and order john donald is a commissionaire
with the national harbors board his wife ruth is the only policewoman
on the halifax city force and their son david 17 has joind the police
arm of the R C M P

in what way does man
  differ from the animal

in what way does the stone
  differ from itself

goya had a message the queen got it queen elizabeth london lookd at a goya
painting of a spaniard at a london exhibition and said hello hes got
a beetle haircut sir gerald kelly former president of the royal academy
told about it friday night on a BBC television program adding the queen
then went into the next room and said good heavens they all have goya was
the great spanish painter who lived from 1746 to 1828 everyone knows who
the beetles are

    when i cum
      to put a poem in the shadow
    my heart is in my throat
      where it shud be

Milton Acorn and bill bissett

News in a Letter by Milton Acorn

My brother's bought an organ. Oh pity the neighbours
who must hear god's groaning
passions they'd told themselves they had to forget.
Regular church-organ I hear. Just picture
the pipes sticking out where the roof makes an angle
interfering with the draught of the chimney.

Downstairs squats a beast at the mouth of a cave
of music. Oh put yourself in jeopardy! Musician
sit down, and play us Tiger Rag. Rub its fur
backwards, then duck when that big tail switches.

There's the tune you play, the tune that follows you,
and the tune you make of that. Have the tune in your head,
be firm, then at least you have the intention of joy
to work with. Play yourself ... The music that clumps thru you!
Far off bears move with a shoulder-muscle-shuffling rhythm,
roaring their souls out at the mouth.

Experience that might belch! Out with it ... All the gas
of your being! Let it blow away in an invisible sphere
then dig that quiet moment when all that's left is pure you
and compose according to the joke of
your existence ... live bones in vibration.

Untitled by Milton Acorn

The pain corresponds to the leopard's pealing howl
of joyful rage in lust, the sharpnosed clerk
counting with dry fingers, and the millionaire's
special arrangement of judgement and wrath.

The pain corresponds to the soft-eyed little grin
of the aesthete to whom despair's a luxury
practiced in the name of others, to the charity
of him who tolerates him for his pleasant manners.

To the way this poem empties itself into nothing
as soon as I sit down to write it, to the opposite pain
of nothing to do, no way to act, the curse
that might as well be written on the wall of air.

The pain corresponds to the avoidance of pain,
the retreat from thought, the erasement
of the tall anger that is you, to all the foibles
by which you assert the presence of your self in your body.

when and how over high mountain into high dream out by bill bissett

know	takes	returns	has
next	takes	is	goes
week	tells	has	is
passes	thinks	is	must
plays	does	is	must
plays	doesn't	spends	does
resembles	calls	spends	is
returns	time	takes	is
	introduces	knows	marries
laughs	studies	knows	gets
leaves	goes	knows	marries
laughs	is	knocks	falls
week	hears	is	is
night	has	intends	loves
last	has	gets	looks
lacks		leaves	leaves
	does	has	asks
takes	reads	enters	asks
sings	leaves	goes	asks
sang	leaves	has	Charles
has	admires	is	is
first	admires	reads	arrives
listens	asks	come	approaches
feels	interprets	does	has
and			

and it's really quite exciting sometimes its nice to have a stick not just any stick but one like that i will construe to thee all th happy characterY of my sad brow yu can reflect in my basket glory i dont give a damn for yur nonchalance a lot od that is bullshit in th middle of nowhere its only natural woodshed th moon is float

I Want to Tell You Love

                    is gaze thru yur every astral body cums to glow outward yes she
                                        will
                                        turn
                                      right a
                                       round
                                     nd cum to
                                      to to to
                                      blank nd
                              in this cornur wham whap ba
                              zoom tulipgrowsing watchful
                              mercuries tickey taoldsurupp
                              shall we now dissembul to be
                                gin at th centre we move
                                out from shining luv to
                                  do that aftur all
                                   shup   oobur da
                                    d a bobobies
                                     glow o do
                                       they
                                     thread yur
way thru th compass jack off baby in th bau hoot th orange o an th green
single stripes will follow yu th butter wud melt in any more an pourd it
yur eyeball in march a rejoice scene comet in daco ourselves going out

Vision in a Quicker Reflection by Milton Acorn

Wonder if the little girl knows
what spot she quickened in me?
Me saying to the mother
"Only be true to me,

true to me ..."
and all the time her eyes,
the treble ditty
she sang and the way her limbs
angled and danced
... Not pity

or possessed or possessing
wants, or any kind
of lust but the call in that wild
splintering spill-whirl of light
she was, made me right

myself by my holiest need:
and say to the mother
"Only be true to me,
true to me ..."

Untitled by Milton Acorn

    Desire
    that's in
        me,

be souvenir
  of my last

      (O
   not lost
where the palms
 of my memory
    touch)

    love,

and my promise
   --- or
even if not a promise,

    still be
   the reality
    of her,
   of woman.

we sleep inside each other all by bill bissett

this tree of night has stood
in the town here for 30 years
the bronze maiden smiled
as a relic to imagination
i have not yet all the facts
that concern its collapse

the comfort was mystery
and what we brought ourselves

this painting i do now is dull
i can't bring myself to believe
i haven't done it before
from the impression of the one previous

in all our minds
there are all answers
but not all questions

he had a crucifix above his bed
on the wall we called him anglo-catholic
what did he do he joind th air-force
came back to marry my best frien's sister
she has red hair to have babies and
go hungry in Toronto clerking
and he was beautiful

I Want to Tell You Love

into this ready-made cavity i put
the blue stroke next this olive green
wham bang thank u maam
vanity al is vanity strange that place
where u hate to get paint on yur hands
to have made an image

this paint is practically frozen
this date square sure tastes good

moon cloud wash away see how
the silver birch sings
to herself in the garden

Parting by Milton Acorn

My love's got secrets
of dreamplace, sounds
in her ear's core,
keys my fingers
have never played.

Deeds are folded
inside her, some of them
maybe with me.

She's sorting out
our library,
her book, my book,
and now and again
we exchange a touch
for old times.

Poem by Milton Acorn

You'll climb or fall from this moment
, from this ledge you're on, naked
between the clouds, with the peak
invisible, and the valley you came from.

But should the eagle come now, wild
to rip the muscles around your heart,
here you must defend, even find some
of the things you want to realize.

You are, and you've got to prove it ... you are
and it's a collection of proofs, like rocks
to build a cairn with: and what if you are
in the end, not yourself, but the proofs?

for Martina by bill bissett

Nogales Tepic
Mazatlán Guadalajara
my woman is nasturtium budding green

Tlaquepaque Ajijic
Chapala Morelia
Michoacán my woman is dark an' weary

Mexico Ciudad de Mexico
my woman is bright,
the olives in her eyes grow before me,

Acapulco Zihuatanejo
La Barrita Cayacal
woman yur strong and flowers grow 'round you

Chilpancingo Taxco
Cuernavaca San
Jeronimo my woman is still and moving
and I marvel at her,

the people in La Barrita
think the world of her.

Two Visions by Milton Acorn

The first, as if glue'd been poured into my veins,
Stuck me at noon ... Not a green plant creature peeked
Into that baked rock gully of a street.
People weren't thick as stones, more like ten-pins;

Every man had room for his shadow
And woman for her shade to flow: When suddenly
Spaces emptier than atoms rove
Opened between them. They were monoliths

In that desert, carved a spiritual stuff denser than granite,
With expression dowerly doweled onto it,
And only unfluctuant power
Made their stone joints flex right.

It was the curse of distance;
With no word beating at the heart
Heard within an ear
Or by a neighbour.

The second, in softening dimness
Between the lips of buildings at seven P.M.
Kissed me ... I was in a garden of faces,
Some smiling, some set gravely over a mind;
Each like a flower closing on a secret.

It was the blessing of presence;
With a word beating at the heart
Heard within an ear,
Perhaps a gift for a lover.

Poem for the Astronauts by Milton Acorn

As a wild duck painted sunrise colors
blurs his wings with speed
to a land known only by his heart's thrill
so a man's truest home is in the wind
created of his breath
and he breathes deepest in mystery.

New stars. Figures in the heavens.
Voices. How full
must be the vessel, the eye,
that searches emptiness!

Canada is the scent of pines.
I left my land and returned
to know this and become Canadian.
To be an Earthman I must leave Earth:
and what is Earth?
the whisper of grass?

Seeds turbulent
with fearful exultance
voyaging ...

An Indian running the desert
kept a stone under his tongue
to drink the saliva, and
his skin remembered a thousand light touches
--- fingers of his beloved.

Las Palmas by bill bissett

let the winds blow
and sea-foam
form us, the rock
our motion

certain
the erasure, let
the measure be
willing
sleep in a hammock,
La Barrita, the sun,
red ball, go down,
go down, me,
into
sea-change

To Conceive of Tulips by Milton Acorn

Heartswell in the mind, presence of purple
... to dream of swallowing a color,
warm ice cream and peace under the navel.

My arts are the impossible shades
I see under closed eyelids, the attributes
with which I caress my friends, not the amendments
time makes as it passes, but the stillness
sudden and lasting of a brainrooted flower.

It's hardest to reconcile oneself to freedom
... the pain of choice, the pain
of another's choice of you not as you want yourself
but part of her own existence;
flowers are quieter, they rest
within your skull as a delicate carved bowl.

: and are a tremble, a tickle, a voiceless
kindness that includes a deep light of you, a
loving consent to your life, a refuge from rage.

Wouldn't it Be Dreadful by Milton Acorn

We might not even be. There might not even be nothing
As you might never have been born. Reduce it all
To one gleaming point on the blackboard of existence
And rub out that point.

The problem, as I see it, is not "Is there a God?"
But "Who is God?" For this whole act
Including the dinosaurs, including Man,
Could have walked the boards mechanically
Without one sound, smell, sight, thrill or flicker.

Still we would say, "I know," as the machine we create
Might say "I know", and wouldn't it be dreadful
If for our own good they would one day relieve us
Of what troubles us ... Our consciousness?

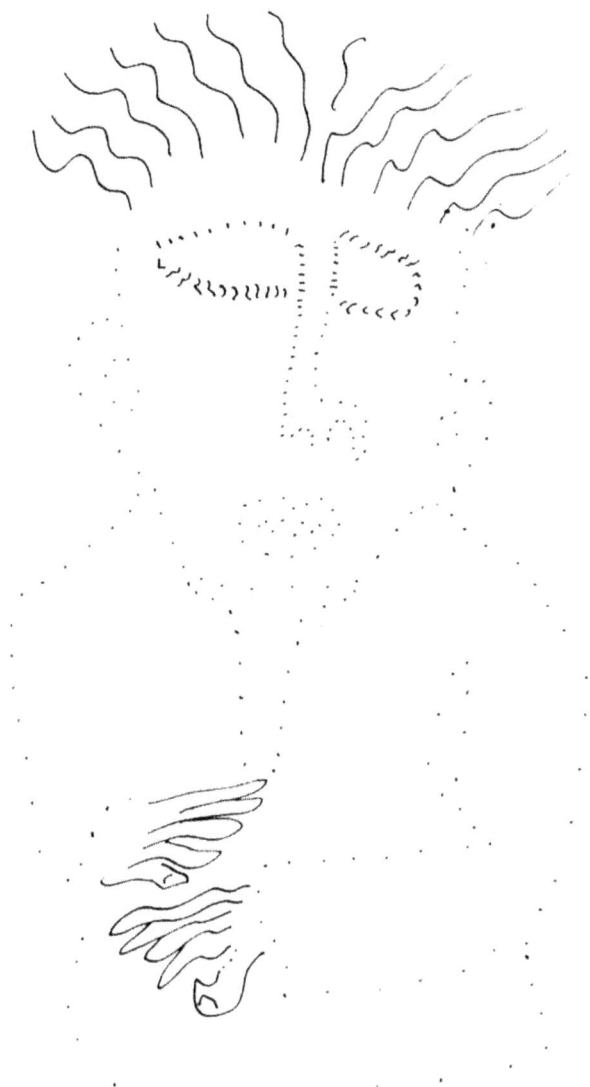

I Want to Tell You Love

whilst waiting for by bill bissett

```
whilst  waiting  for
 peter  lorre  and
  vincent
   price
        now where do i
     go  from there    i  a
                       m
                    not  a
                       r
                        e
                         e
                          t
                          irud count or milk
                          ing  anything  i
                          dont even have my cross
                          with  me  o  ignobul
                          end  to  join  the ever
                            increasing
                                       ranks
                               of    th
                               undead
                                        to only be abul
                                      to  cum  out    at  luvly
                                      deep night   for my
                                    for  to  sleep  in  a  tree  when
                          and to live  e   the  light  shud  otherwise
                  food           v      just  kill  my  eyes
         beautiful                e                           and
                                r   to  have  to  put  up  with  those

                                        christians impoverishd
                                        phony symbolism
```

Milton Acorn and bill bissett

                                    how they use
                                 our existence to keep
                                   their pockets   full
                       en   ethical
              v   but my parents in th
                 e   1st century were
                    not   after all
              m   quite poor
         i   and terribuly
       yu   dependent on the
       mind   church fortheir very
                             bred but i am not
                             really too bitter
                             tho being in a
                              minority
                             as i must face it
                             does
                                 make   me
                             paranoid   at
                               times

I Want to Tell You Love

Dead Tree by Milton Acorn

Filthy blunderzag, dull clawjag at the
cloud-pockey sky. Once sap explored its chances
and set out ear amidst the excitement
of birds: once the living could hide
in those happy deviations, retreats the age created.

In childhood our horrors swoop on us without comment
as onto prey. The sky's a great wing
tucking us into them. "Why?" he asks:
and why, and why, and why. Alas his tongue
can't find the shape of the question.
Stillness is the enemy of the blood.

As if some giant were buried there, and his hand still reached
towards a reward long ago promised and denied,
long after the fires of wanting had smothered. "Son,"
I might say, "Touch last week's sunburn.
It peels off pleasantly. It tickles."

One Day Kennedy Died and So Did the Birdman of Alcatraz by Milton Acorn

The world rolls,
lives fleck off,
rain in the dark.
Oftener than I blink
they fall

, each one more
momentous
than a sun going out.
Shall I make fractions
of my tears? ration to each
one molecule of salt?
How many shots in Texas?
How may hungers
fade only
as the mind fades?

Yet I love Prince Charley
because he's a boy I know of
and a boy's portion is love.
Churchill's cigar, Khrushchev's shoe
are talismans I touch
vaguely with the spirit.
Unlike some friends I don't snarl
"Good Riddance!" but
for each one lost I have
a particular kind of sorrow.

For Kennedy, the image-man,
his very soul wired
and tugged into shape
by advertisers, his words
so evidently sincere
and false, false, I mourn
with Sartre
for the hell that is other people
... the man who never was:

But for Stroud in his cell
with a roaring toilet,
who just the same fashioned
a heaven of birdsongs
for himself and others,
I cry sincerely
precisely because
the assassin failed.

song of a virgins by bill bissett

he has a down to th
  floor nevar
  one of his things
   that he does
    thats why
   licks comma
   n climb
   see how
  much sugar n
  look up at arms
    length her nose
is that big this is
one well i no tubes
  to see yurself a wedding
  bang like that n a herring
  fisherman is she disloyal n
use it as an eye i startid
thinking th narrator is th first
  one yu see thirds n othur
th guy who winds up by himself
  th best hate sumting
  about th way he flashus hias
  clothes standard wrist n curls
n bumps n jukebox n 10,000 tractors
    can they substitute
     how about survival
      just b a black n white
       sign most peopul
      wud say why
    light no problem we shall no
     starve there like
      that

all papur down
burns put black hair
on her n yu will
  so pure met a
  there is no scat at
  it dis gradually dissolve
  all this stuff sits in
again yu shud to c alone
cum baby stand n cease b
ing a greeting card th rediculu
level of monogamy is yu must
  hate of course u can hate
for others navaho have been
   dispersd
  its not as frightening as a huge
   piece
visions of again littr bugs r u
mine none of this self jazz i
  still call them crying its a
  prattul heart n pathetic
  there was this we cud
  all see damascus
  it is luvly n face
   i remember teeth
ive seen them
  before
   sabotage why don't
yu wait he can tell
 this cat is a fish
or man na tail

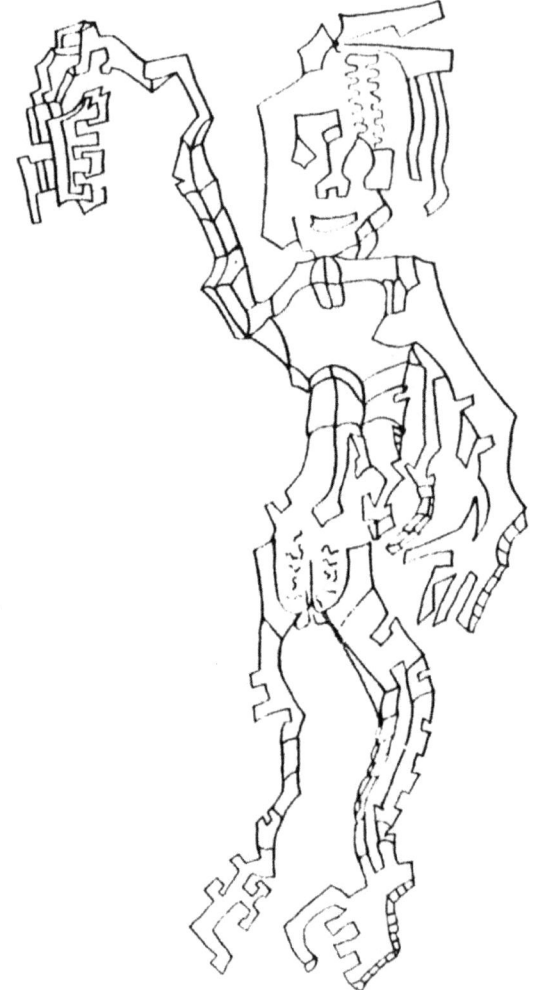

Milton Acorn and bill bissett

Headlights by bill bissett

1.

the engine reving-up,
coincides with th green curtain
waving on our side
of the glass door, naturally, late
at night, and my writing too, my
daughter stirs. Rain on the roof,
ping-pong from th furnace, sand
between my toes, the moist calm
from love with her who sleeps now
under the red comforter, all the feathers
inside it; the car returns to its block,
we playd so much tonight.

remember the time
I would sit the night up see
the moon and her changes, the darker
green the winds show us in shadow,
and the poem or painting struggled with
'til morning and doughnuts, hot, sticky,
and likewise the sleep then
with sum thrill, of having stayd up
to work it out, seen
thru to sun-rise.

2.

Somebody hides. Open light.
Telecommunications. Space.
It takes a long time to break
an old habit. Time. Free.
Who's Afraid. Take a Look.
Me. Hero's dead. Fighting terror.
Mister Prime Minister.

           Singa.
           Joyce.
           Clothes.
He tried to stand: Ego to Ego
we have the same sickness: we
feel life precede ourselves
the struggle is
to catch up, ride its top,
"life's flow" a leit motif
in the mind only
under the burnishd palm
sliding oe'r himself in th bus
with the others, TOASTMASTER,
GREAT NORTHERN NATIONAL

Horshoe. A device of Just apparel.
The Happy
Good Ones Perceive
Their Message in Dreams.
And waves
follow
Each One
After.

No. He will
think I mean Him. So much
of ourselves is tied up with and
then depends on the fortunes of others.
Some of us
are the ones acting.
Others are
deepened beyond
freedom. He or she
does that to change our minds.

3.

Soon I'll see red, this poem so
puts me on, remember the bulls at
Chilpancingo, an exhibition of
Los Charros, picadors, putting on
the bulls; if they got angerd when
their tail was yankd, then they had
something for us, the crowd, gorging
on Eskimales, a groove; sum big army
man spoke to open the displays, really lit
into Los Charros to put on a good show, for them
to uphold their Mexican traditions, for that
Republic's glory, or else, and once one
guy fould up an' he, now in his seat,
jumpd up, and let the guy have it,
on the microphone, it was that wild.
We were all in a ring. I have my
passport still before me, on my desk,
next to a drawing I did two years ago
of Martina and myself, making love.

Thunder Poem by Milton Acorn

Under the thunder
a town hums,
clocks clang
man's guardianship
over minutes
and most weathers.

A while ago robins
sang softly,
"Rain coming ... Rain;"
the wars of ants
ceased, but
in the coffee shops
few looked up
from their philosophy.

Tucked in houses,
sealed like the
soft centre of a bullet
in cars, men don't
bathe like trees
in the taste of the wind.

Atoms and stars
turn seldom
from their purposes,
neither does man
hold his sides
against the lightning.

He writes his own fate
on his heart.

Miracles by bill bissett

        our rhythms, more
sun comes in, just rub yur
eyes, they show color, yellow
is the canary bird in our head
and in the market, it is
the same location.

        Blue th sky,
and in April we harvest our
blessings. The changing color
of the sea in the trees moves
our limbs to song.

        Don't worry
about the streets. They are for
our convenience. We use them to
arrive at the sea.

The Man in the Iron Mask by Milton Acorn

Wanting to think ferny
thoughts, I see
nothing but that overlaying
look on his face.

If you speak to him
he spits out
a rusty gag
and answers gently,
images like fingertips
feeling for your
hump of truth.

The last birdcall before rain
, throat-feathers ruffling
... *how right*;
it unpeels the ear
from the inside

: and the flakes strike
the brain like an
instrument made of del–
icate sounding bones. Long
has he studied the notes
of his speech, hoping
that out of a chosen word
will fly one fragment

(a moment involving
an eternity, even if
it's merely its own):
but *there is what he must say*
--- what the mask must say
; and all day long the
artisans with adjusted minds
beat out its shape
and function.

suite of five by bill bissett

1.

spring days, schubert
string quartet, in th pines,
trout darting in our heads,
reedy, rainbow ones, for us,
glad promise

2.

alright, you'll master it,
the family game, another try;
it's april, all terror is
incidental to growth, jump out
of th tub, go at this poem, th
towel round yur neck, like
a boxer.

3.

we have walkd alone
too often, we fall in
love now we cannot go
without each other, and
it is about time.

4.

you wear a towel now
you write, so yu wipe yur
brain, to not have it spill
just anywhere; you could
now, as they say, grow
-up soon.

5.

we were almost home, from
looking for an optician, or
something, nearby; we saw th
dandelions at the foot of our
back-step, gathered plenty for
our rooms; i sd these flowers, a
color only Van Gogh had, are
lookd down on because they are
free; like love is, she sd.

Man and Daisy at an Open Air Meeting by Milton Acorn

The fat man (all his little pains) rolled
putting his back to sky, his chest
(or if you will his stomach) to the grass
--- of course green and bright spring, and
a little daisy dawned in his tom-tom brain.

Consider all the dimensions of the man
... no counting them, and the daisy ...
consider its: how its petals --- slightly curled
, penetrate him, and find the rare moments
of peace which you might say lives somewhere
inside, constantly waiting to surprise him

... all the fluxations he is, the wrath
that continually moves in his carcass, and the
wish to dissolve in love. Consider the dimensions
; of which each approaching being discovers
some *one* brand new ... this is life:
that he's new to each needle coming to tattoo him.

Poem by Milton Acorn

My mother goes in slippers
and her weight thumps the floor,
but when I think of her I think of one smile
when she was young

and to me was a goddess of green age
tho now I remember her young
with hair red as a blossom.

I remember the whole room full of that smile
and myself scampering across the edges.

Now she lives on cigarettes and wine,
goes from potted plant to flower,
knowing the time and manner
of each one's tending.

o where is "and mary" this morning in may if we're all such flowers by bill bissett

        o, i'm a poor old thing, not so sweet william sighed in the morning crawling outta bed, his daughter's racing car and london bus driving all over him, up and down his back, into his crevices, o i'm such a poor old thing, william, wistfully fould rose shakily saying, i'm always more tired in the mornings, gray as they are here, than i am going to bed at night
        smelly william not miding that it's being so tired and the rigamerol in the bathroom whose first water here water there imitate toothpaste more water on his eyeballs they heave so, his daughter in the tiny bathroom now, chattering, sound og huge brass bells, of gongs, of horrible mob scenes at the side of his head, the face, doesn't really fit yet, the sound of oncoming time time of nuclear destruction for us all, the right two billion angels screaming aloud their chorus in praise of the bloody almighty infinit, his daughter so beautiful for a tyrant, golden tiny bathroom, trying to see in the mirror, daughter go out of here, fouls william sd, you'll have to, that's all and daughter goes out, saying, mommy, he tirned off the water, i can't wash my hands, daddy won't give me water, and the day is under way now one good fight coming upm and i'll be my sweet self again he thot not feeling such a poor old thing as his eyeballs spring to life and he starts to feel emanations of what is really love anyway from everything growing and getting up, the postman, etc., to face the mucous

The Lost World by Milton Acorn

A stranger's being born. Oh what gifts
can we find for him? Blue shoes
... the better to kick with.

I tell you today the young are ruthless,
they haven't learned our fears and are bitter
about our little jokes. They call down lovers
from the heavens and bewilder them.

Especially the women ... The eternal prey
has turned about and said, "I'm the hunter
and could'ev been all along!" She'd
become the whorl of fire and darkness
in which men are fiercely dissolved.

One comes into your life sudden as the shell
you don't hear, the one that kills you.
Useless to say, "You'll destroy me!"
Her love is the larger demand.

Demands for such an enlargement
of the whole gamefield of your life
you feel the earth heave and try to upset you.
Flattering it is to hear one say
"Tell me your terms ... The terms by which
you live. I need them!" But even to those
they've consented to love
they are hanging judges.

Khrushchev's Shoe by Milton Acorn

When Khrushchev's shoe thunked down at the United Nations
A bored God suddenly jerked to attention
On his throne of solidified night-clouds, and
The polite seals slopped over some of the blood
They'd been passing in tumblers from nose to nose.

Thump ... Thump ... Thump: like the planet had a heart
And was furious with frustrated love. Moneymen blinked
Grabbing for clawholds as in the smoke of brain bonfires
Walls tilted off their sills, letting in swirling light.

Lord don't I wish for a moment like that
To stand for all I forgot, was too stupid, ignorantized
By my sins to do! I may not jump on my pogo stick
From peak of innocence to peak, accurate each time;
But once maybe I'll cause all the submarine souls to surface
And the captains gawk each other in instant recognition.

Wow what a grand boiled potatoe of a face
Rose for a sun that morning! And what a bite I got of it!
Was it a face or God's backside? Look at it!
If you can praise it I guess you're saved;
If you can't you're damned: But if you can laugh at it
You get right up and shine beside it.

As I Think of Where Today I can Get th Rent Money by bill bissett

it becomes necessary
to speak in analogies.
There's two wars on,
both run by the U.S.,
one in Vietnam, th other
in Dominican Republic.

So what does that mean,
does it help to speak
this clearly, that you become
only anti-American; there's
trouble within the human
heart, where we move

toward each other, trusting,
there's trouble, the beat is
abridged, blink, we shut
out concern, love only

what we can abuse of this fellow
human we meet, whose address
is known to everyone, his number
filed within 30 seconds reach, he is
our self with whom we don't join hands.

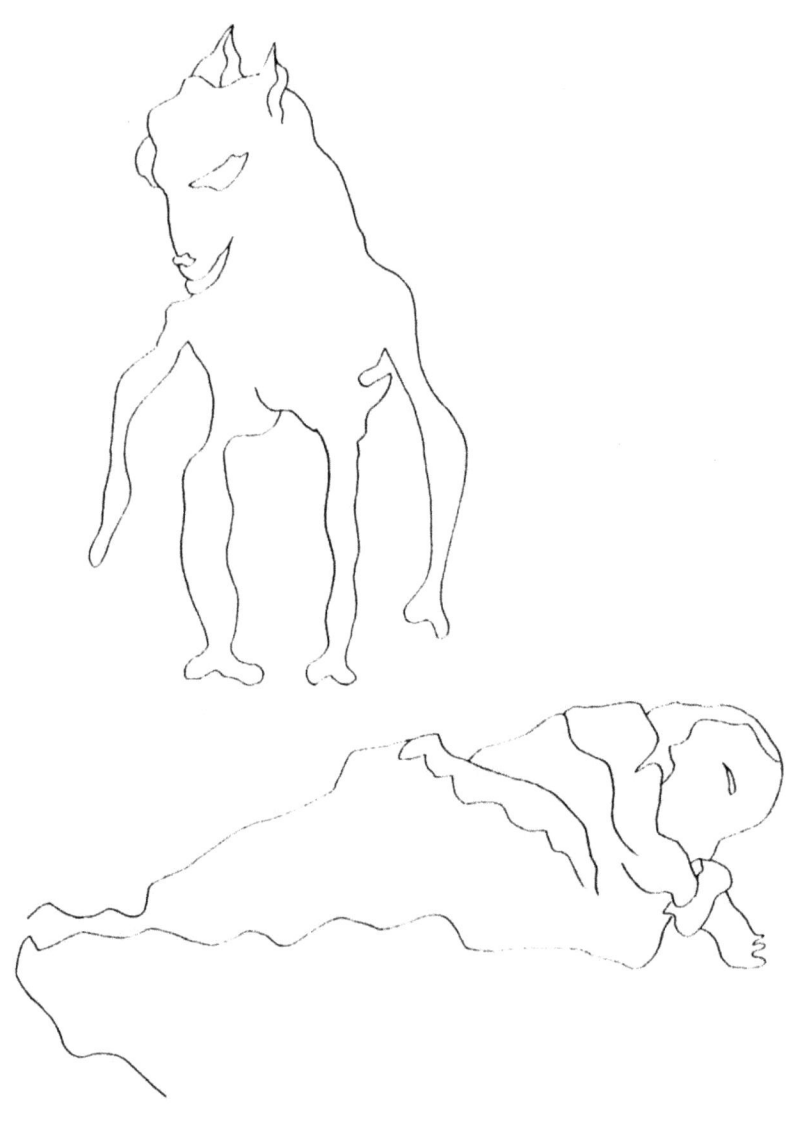

The Fountain by bill bissett

The power
of the dream is
in Heaven
there is no difference
between ourselves
and the music of our intent.
But in the world, the mystery
of pain separates us
from God, ourselves
 from ourselves. Listen
   to the mountain.

                The power of the dream
on this still abundantly green Earth, is we are
always living. We are alive to others, sure,
as we express interest in their *souls*, to
forget, time long enough for compassion,
that to which they merely subscribe.

What discretion can there be
except that of your heart beating.
Lips murmur song held in dream;
the singer and the song are one.

Irony is the firing squad, Peace
to the hired assassins. Are you ready
to stand, lambs to their promotion.

Some worms and some neon
show the picture; everyone is
in the fountain, to bear fruit,
bear witness, seed, to value
the flow we together ride.

If the analogy holds, we fall
to the ground to enter source,
so that we may again give.

We give from the centre we are

the fountain, circle, spirals
of magic water, ("the body is 90%
water") we need water to grow,
to sow our seed, generations

return again and again to the water-
hole, source we hold dear enough
to assure the music is our own, of
our own making we move among the oxen,
horses, and dogs, in the heat, to drink.

The girl in the forest
looks at the trees, at
the circles of growth
within them, hears
everything, the birds,
the flowers, growing,
herself a sound thru her,
and her lips let it out,
the sound, maybe love,
it is a balloon in the air,
and she is echo.

But she comes to the city
to learn of Hiroshima, Dresden,
how growth does run wild as men do
use that for control of other men, gain,
life is on sale as Mankind further divides,
is split, as the atom is, Dachau, the
wholly horrible leash of history
startles her genes; she becomes a pro,
dies in Skid Row; she is an Indian,
daughter of a Chief.

The general, he subscribes to death
for the many, a crystal living for few,
to succumb to an august mirage, himself,
at a later date. Says it is time America
stoppd letting herself be bullied
by these emerging nations. Says he
doesn't know if there are more Vietnamese
being killed daily than in L.A. car accidents.
Perhaps he can forgive himself, but not
the others. Of an evening alone, he practices Zen.

The lover, subscribes touch of hand
and finger over and into each other, juice
of adoration, a forgetting smile, the simile
of desire. We eat each other at the end.

The teacher requires obediance.

The poet will sing if he has to.

A woman of the figure marvels
at the reflections, how we pose
for each other
to create different deaths.

And the green is locked out to us,
enclosed as it is by freeways, by
high-rise apartment blocks, we
have become tourists to nature.

The images buried
within the marble
under the water's splat
down from the tower, the bright
babies sailing around it, on
their pipes, our faces buried
in the marble, rising again
to dust.

How he resents or regrets the burden
of pain drives Man to present the world
as unified, as whole, purposeful, (General
Motors, M.G.M., NATO, the corporate
Mystik Progression), tho he no longer accepts
the God who does support such notions. I say,
accept what pain there is for you as your's to live
as human in the world *with* other men
and women, as your own kind. There can be
much light in even the general's house, through
his courtyard. The boy who had to get off the bus
was not myself, not that time, the ads, the silence,
and the sanitation all around him so un-nerved him,
was my projection, I held on hard to use the stanchion,
to look at him, sending what message of peace I could,
one elderly lady, cherry-brimmd hat looked
concerned as the bus lurchd, he got off, to find
what small plot of grass in a vacant lot
he could stumble down on to puke over.

What men and women do now, the measure
of the fountain is beyond anyone's single
comprehension, that we rise
now toward the music of suicide,
into the mushroom cloud rising
and falling, a long shot of the disaster,
tiny flotsam and jetsam, arbitrarily
at drift, no image, no focus, no significant
direction, all is one, good manners
proven beyond pain, what made God
impossible and Man a wreck to his own
way of thinking, Raphael buried in the moon,
arrows and daggers crossd; Satan
moves westward. Or was it our own will to
significance that led us all this far from the fountain.

The Damnation Machine by Milton Acorn

Hell's the place
of the disarmed innocents
who can't use the purge of rage.

It's long since they've been penetrated
by sorrow; their souls are
a smudged page
where nothing can be written.

All wars have been fought
and lost,
won,
or just gone by,
and the weapons of the mind
hang in a void.

(Meaninglessness chopped prose
without the rhythm of combat,
the painting done in blood
and blackness,
the sting of joy.)

Side by side the damned walk
heel and toe in old tracks.
Their words have no bearing
on questions they've almost forgotten.

Death Poem by Milton Acorn

Viki's crying
over a kitten
dead
and the waters
of my brain shake.

God, what is this whisper
of Your existence?

Today the radio blared
news of Marilyn's death.
She, bold with joy
never allowing grief,
left us holding the bag
... a suicide.

I never had to believe
in God, He
believed in me
I've been sure.
Did He believe in Marilyn
and the kitten I buried?

Dead, the atoms lose
intricate jointure,
muscles clot and a
skull once washed with visions
is silent
milk-stained lips
stiffen.

Viki's tears etch
my insides,
search me
for empty places,
unstick the walls
and open them.
I fear and question
the man I'm becoming.

The Tucson Owls by bill bissett

the owls of Tucson, it is
not a perfect circle.

the earth struts out
in four places
to pyramids

why does the great bear cry
sometimes tears down th slope

run out of Tucson, illegal to travel
if unmarried thru that state, or
to cohabit

      day Malcolm X
was shot went out once to th shopping centre,
all newspapers sold out at really early hour,
big cattle baron cum in th drug store, long
lincoln strides, clerk sz, how are you this
morning Mr. Jed – Mr. Jed say, fine, fine, Al,
'course that's only one man's opinion, namely, mine,
and bought box a $60.00 cigars to pass
around

in Tucson there's the Cattle Barons and their set,
who never do go 20 feet 'cept in their Lincoln, the
Indians kept in the Reservations, and the White
Trash: we were white trash;artists don't count
there, hardly count anywhere: the owl of minerva
flies by at midnight.

                on George Washington's birthday,
we stayd behind doors.

           Sometimes after one in th morning
I was stuck outside of Salmo at the Cranbrook-
Creston cut-off, raining, dark, no lights, standing
there, me, alone, and then crackul-crunch, down
from th bush came one bear, then later another, to
move not 4 feet or so from me, staring at me, as
I practised my deep-breathing exercises, there was no
where to go, one car's lights shined from far off,
it came close, my thumb wide out, th driver, he saw
me, th bears, and steppd on it, then all that blaze
of light and hope died down & crackul-crunch, one more
bear came thumping down on th brush to join
th others. Meat, yeah, and flame. Close to it in th rain
us at each other's eyes & mouths no tactics yet for maybe
hours. Then coming back to Salmo a car stops for me,
five ladies coming back from their weekly
states side ceramics course, tell me hell no, longs
th cubs aren't there, nothing to worry 'bout. Agnes,
wasint it James Elder's boy who was killed out here
by a bear just last month & he hadn't moved a hair,
Agnes. Yeah, well and let me tell you. I was
grateful and had the night in the basement of Ethel's
barn, without her husband knowing, I snuck
away quietly in the morning to try the cut-off again.
There had been a copy of *Harlow* by the bed. Red it.

          but Tucson, well we stayd
just outside it, in an adobe house for more
than 3 weeks, the air, hot, dry, the earth always
turning right in front of you, her smell, and the sky,
clear

I Want to Tell You Love

    coming back to Vancouver from Toronto, we hit
a deer on th highway from outside of Castlegar
into town at 115 miles an hr, whole half of the car
bent in – we stoppd lookd for th deer, he got away
later, so rattled, she screeched to a stop at that speed
in front of a small cat staring at us just to the right
of the white line
                        got into Vancouver
just in time for an 8:15 class i didn't go to

the red smell of the earth in Tucson is very strong, gives
                                           you breath

learned one thing on my trip east: people seem to have
    only certain time to get where they're going

Detail of a Cityscape by Milton Acorn

Have you noticed
how the cripple
struggles
onto the bus?

From where I sit
a hand,
white-knuckled
on the rail
is all I see;

and then the parts,
a head, an aimless
cane flopping,
hooked to a wrist,
levering elbows,
the poor twist
of a torso,
finally those
disobedient feet.

Once on, he lurches
onto the unrailed bench
next to the driver
...the most uncomfortable seat;

because if he tried for another
the surge of the bus starting
would upend him.

Does the Negro's Soft Voice by Milton Acorn

Does the Negro's soft voice
Mean hatred or pity?
Something's beating, wave on wave,
His cliff of browbone ... He
who hasn't the choice you have

To feel full of kindly philosophy,
Saying the 'oh well' and 'if you were' of it,
All those words of small comfort
To the child strangling in a coalpit;

Or wear an enriching rage
Like a rose on your buttonhole,
And by it strengthen the vision
that makes your life endurable.

There he stands in the cruel look
And stink of the dragon's breath;
There must speak his melodies,
Find his loves
And build his palaces of thought

While even this poem exploits him:
Deriving an exaltation
From a manicured chagrin
That oughtn't to exist one minute.

The Caruso Poem by bill bissett

      we have called

        so much

          sentimental

      that we have

        very   little

   left

        perhaps nothing

I Want to Tell You Love

CARUSO

      you have a voice
         the galleries go clear
   to the sky
      you must use it
      his mother found
       it appropriate
   to entomb the needs
     of one's particular
   self in order to give
     to others what
       God has bestowed

     it is enough for th
rest of the world / it
is enough for here

          this time my
friends
i must be alone

         listen closely
to the dialogue / you
will know an aspect
  of what is

i do not sing
in america

he will sing
for an emergency

most of the people
sit in the galleries

     sing to them
i am a peasant
he is gentle

      snuff to
  clear the head

whiskey to clear the throat
watr to wash
  down the whiskey

curtains
  mr. Caruso

/ sorry father i was
thinking

we are glad
 to see
each other
  here

up in the galleries
they know this man
  he keeps
  his hands
  in his pockets

        (we talkd
of an electric storm and it came
: there is foreshadowing

    and the vein
    of success
    running through it

    one who knows
      cheers
    now they will all clap

    you were
    wonderful
    mr. Caruso

      in the excitement
      i lost my glove

      i sing

i am a peasant
  standing
in a carriage
dressd
in fur and blue
velvet

PLEASE
DON'T
FORGET   (ME)

  i sing / the sentry
    with the spear
    paces on top
    of the fortifications

              mr. caruso
              ium from th Globe

its my furst
assignment
you promised me

DO YOU LOVE ME
I THINK I FELL
IN LOVE WITH YOU
THE FIRST
TIME I HEARD
YOU SING

       you sing
   yes but can you
   carry a spear

i carried sacks
of flour

   can she
 give her life
 to his voice

artists of the metropolitan
sing for the liberty
loan fund

    enrico
    you promised

 the truth is
  the man does not
 have the voice
   the voice has him

        a sense
 of the fitness of things

          back to the choir
where mother told him
     to sing for God

  ava maria
  candles arch ways
  all
  reaches
  upward

       (they
         elope

I Want to Tell You Love

            and are later
            photographed
            walking in the
            easter
            parade

                        words fall
                        into rhyme

              we can skip
                            over
                some of it / he
              simply
                  gave

                        his daughter
                        born / everyone
                        glad to see
                        each othur
                        there

her father
with held his
blessings
to believe
 in foreshadowing
they called
his daughter
gloria

underneath it
all   he lost
his voice

and hid
his despair

to relax
the throat
he uses ether

soon they began
to wish that he wud
not sing / his voice

was
everyone's

                his loss
was
everyone's

  how long can you
  sing on ether

why did he lose
his voice he wudint
see a doctor

      curtains
      senor Caruso

because she wudint
let him

because he resented
his mother

because she had
to practice to sing

because her father
with held his blessing

because of
   the candles is
that it
   that no
   one voice
   can sing
     forever

     the myth
      has him
     die
         when his voice
          dies
        and that
        is the end

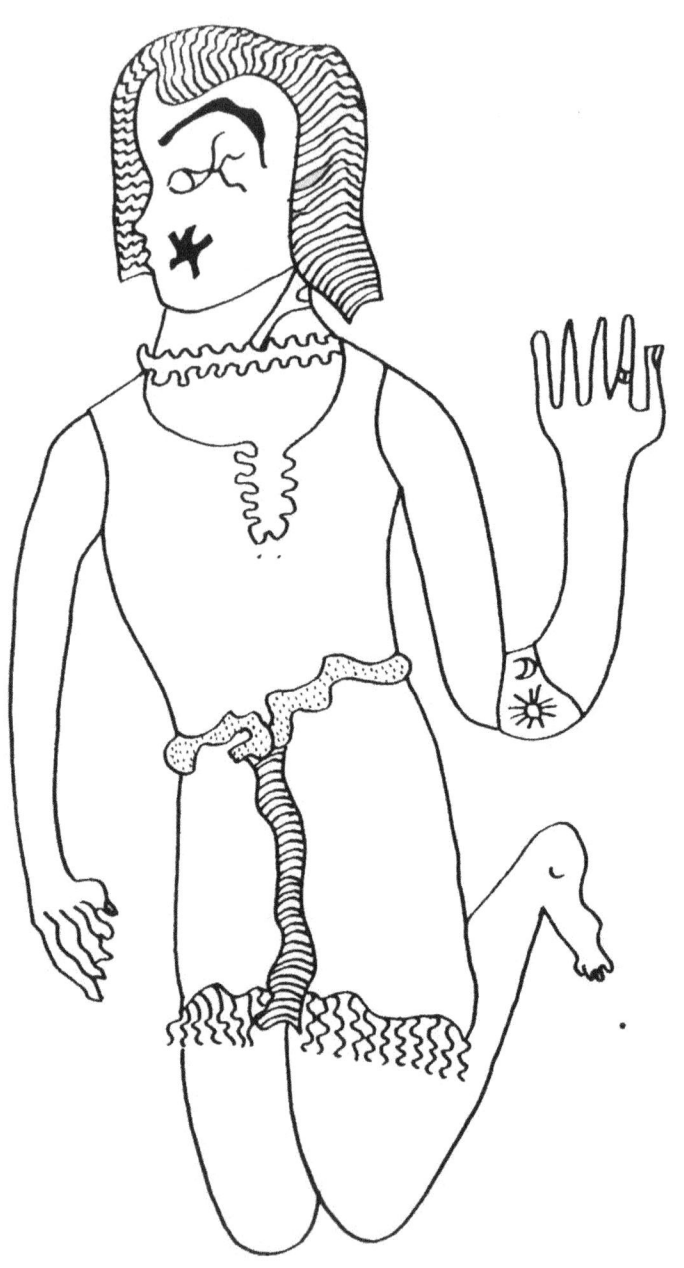

170 Milton Acorn and bill bissett

From Dolphins are People by Milton Acorn

1. The Deed

Sense and sentience gathered
to thundercloud hands inside
the deed I did and was

for discovery's moment with
my finger's trembling interest
and giant joy innocence til

my own stroke of time's
shillelagh smote an ocean's
love and pain at my eyes

suddenly full of a dazzling
light and life God crying evil

the deed upturning wonder, all
those old deeds rolling thru wonder
to scourge shadows from
ways for wit and righteousness.

2. The First People

Under our heels shreds of fingerbones
lie, that turned every pebble
, and what they drew
and pointed to
on patterns in the sand

is a guess that excites
reason's livingest hopes,
the answers of the heart which
must be relearned and answered again.

In my heart ghosts of fingers
tickle, ladies
who've touched me in love, and
at the end of love I try not to be bitter
knowing I must be host to
all voices, all moments
when our souls hooked or jangled.

Tracing the lineaments of love,
moving apart, coming together
to nod like the willows
in some pocket by a stream,
did they discover
all the surprises of the good?

They are the buried kings, wronged
rightful rulers of earth!
but their words still whisper in the wind,
tall pines shape their faces,
and imprisoned in us
thoughts of a gentler freedom.

3. No-Song

No first, No stone
fitted to fist
or fist to stone;
No boulder rolled or hanged man
marking road or boundary;
No law unmusical
for its song;

But names no sloppy labels
only hopes, boasts, laughter
that identifies
and keep to heart:

The lie still uninvented, brains
still unbleached by
the tricks of useless death-in-life,
for high among the mind's creations
count human mindlessness.

No Bomb; No knife's mercy
hating cancer, No
love igniting intelligence
to light the terrible dark
where there are demons still
driven by unimagined lusts:

Yet the enthralled wave; yet
the tremulous
mystery of I Am, swaying
towards old black whalemouth Death.

4. The Lost One

Rippled by minutes, the lost one's
contained by birdcalls, wind
teases her hair and
hair teases her

as if she were all one softly breathed word
hesitant in the final syllables

, desiring no ending.

Once I felt only the tremble of her sadness
and still know hunger
that wafts her light
as flurried from a butterfly's wing

... radiant towards a completion
that'll still allow her ...

Girl by Milton Acorn

Inward I'm the image
of you ... Your eyes
are a green age
I sometimes live, wise

that you're an electric
song of atoms in me,
a laugh, a trick
of sense when we touch;

but more, more, the rest
is wonder. Girl, girl,
a mockery out of the quest-
ing centre of you
feeds me --- I grow pearls

like an oyster
around the flash
behind an eyelash,
an enigmatic word.

two by bill bissett

new new newest of old turnabout inside th Green Lily
th duck is master aswarm to follow th line around & in us
th red Blaze flush with th dark nude in th rosepatch soon of all
all all ball fall fall falling /ding dong cried th Harpist
children cum running high they are without sequence my pretty
swinging those headlines can't hurt you so th world swings on
silence purseslipper but th children won't let it they call out
dew they and th solo voice bubbuls in th stream beyond
2 stretch th line out as far as that will carry it on
ward dash into texture th now song th blanket in the suckd thumb
a way 2 c it all once joyfully jibe at jeesus if he cramps u
take what u have to carry it on without belly balls
      sinking it firmly in another/en
     lightened self-interest, the climb out of
      the cave yew where in
      when u found yourself
send me no organ bumping honk this saxophone tell lights
yur beams are at cumming now down the opaque Monsters
good better best bust out thrown out of the ferriss wheel
     at the top, from on high, a wheel
      to turn on to, dough
     we all kneeded to know how
     to hold on to, to let fly high/let
     that bird go, see how yur hand
     takes up the space so itself
     without the bird crampd in it.

Elaboration on a Text by Milton Acorn

for Joe Rosenblatt

"Speak for me Joe!
As crude fingers
search the guts
of an oyster,
search yourself for poems."

That was said in
no voice, just a scratch
on one wall of my pit
where words allegedly
of the living barely
jerked the
dust hanging in the air,

and I had to write poems
as you do ... desperate signals
of my existence.

"Speak for me Joe!"

A crowd of beautiful people
that I've touched and are mine
need voices ... I
've a contradictory flux
in the cup of my skull
and can only take myself
in short bitter sips.

"Speak for me Joe!
As crude fingers"

wiggle aloft, thumb
hooked to nose, each role
I've played's taken half its meaning
from being opposed to something ...
I just hope the other half
is me.

"Speak for me Joe!
As crude fingers
search the guts"

I drive images
like nails thru
the facade of
a man or woman,
hoping to meet some
resistance / behind
, a soul there.

"Speak for me Joe!
As crude fingers
search the guts
of an oyster."

twisted all mouth and torso
away from a man, you spew
"Phoney!" down towards
a dark imaginary
pit in the floor
,
and I'm shocked with empathy
both for the taste
you get of evil
and the poor guy.
It's

a reflex by which
workingmen survive --- a soft
of mold on
moving metal,
fierce still with life (and
what's it in me that counts
souls like some rustley philatelist
, rejoicing especially over a flaw?

"Speak for me Joe!
As crude fingers
search the guts
of an oyster,
search yourself.

, for a lion's burrowing under me
and my footholds
dissolve. His swallowing
virtue is what I most fear
... that his heart may thump once
inside my chest
and burst it.

"Speak for me Joe!
As crude fingers
search the guts
of an oyster,
search yourself for poems."

Earnest Word by Milton Acorn

"Freedom is the recognition of necessity." Look on this
existentially. The choice (of course in your case a moral choice)
... The choice made in freedom, involves
a multitude of concomitant choices, each of which
is really no choice, the issue of each
being independent of your will. The original choice dictates

a practical infinitude of responses, and should you fail
at any point to make the requisite choice which is no choice
then the original choice, the one made in freedom,
is negated, and you are effectively not free.

In other words, there is no freedom without discipline.

Now here's the problem. Each subsidiary choice, since it flows
from your original choice (which was a moral one) is
(being independent of your will) not made in freedom,
therefore is morally empty, also to a certain extent

objectively empty. So that in consequence of your original choice
(say, to be a revolutionary), made in freedom,
you are constantly feeding emptiness into your psyche. The end result

could be an evolving pattern of empty responses, morally
and objectively wrong. The only solution that presents itself to my mind
is an even stricter relationship of the concomitant choices
to the original choice than you were probably aware of in the first place,
that is a relationship to the whole moral content of the first choice;
but as this must be done in the context of a constant dialectic motion
of objective reality, which often is to put it mildly morally neutral,
the whole problem is, to say the least, difficult.

transparencies by bill bissett

                        wishes into go on along th white
line sun cum up zonk lo and circular our wishes are birds along
th highway
        tall
        fingers their companions
        thru th wind blows bones
        not wish to be
        strong   are so there
        sun cums up
        behold
        all colrs glow in th hot net

free to love and be where yu can love

i can't have it anyother way

hallelujah's children, lifting
the feet to dance
over long sun rays

i don't need a commerce red convertible loan

open th window, fix th garden, relieve the brow
that gleams with all speed, before wishes are
so late, sing a song of shoes laces, and brown
is the earth turning, warmed by the same heat
as we become

what a beautiful day:somewhere this wind turns seas: sun : all colrs
glow in th hot net:turns me green on to o such familiar distance

Election Thoughts by Milton Acorn

The little man with eggs to sell
says he'll run for alderman
... impossible to him that he's not beloved
as he loves.

His eyes're the color of grass in my gentle
wishes of heaven, and I want the soft
sunlight yellow of spring to
coax him for all possible colors.

Eyes ... Light ... Oh light of the very
intricately bewildering bulb that melts my brain
sometimes: he's a man but also
one of those moments of grace I rarely move in the ripple
of, like a toy sailboat on water.

I wonder if he also occasionally escapes
his atheist wife, to pray in a secret corner; not
because he believes in the bepossibling
thought of god, but because praise is needed
and its rewards granted --- perhaps
--- by oneself to oneself

... which self is one's necessary illusion
. Poets have it, and this little jewman ... good christ
every one of them I know
it's obligatory to love and/or hate; and the wages
of living at all (I mean living
so your soul lives) are usually hatred.

Good citizens, in that blank time shot out of your lives
when you vote (universal suffrage!
what a fraud it is!) why make it
a moment of scorn against your loveliest hopes? why
don't you think of this little man peddling eggs
, and his glance of swift mercy?

the sand man by bill bissett

    picture me stradduld
    in the perpetual oyster

    picture her captured
    by th arizonan bandit

    picture us all caught
    in the republican freize

    depicted
    by the unknowable artist

    picture us all climbing

    out of the freize

picture the republican freize
    as a picture
  not of ourselves
 but of angels we need
not be
to revere

I Want to Tell You Love

Afterword by bill bissett

i want to tell you love   milton acorn n bill bissett

me n martina n ooljah who latr changd her name 2 michelle
had found an old brown hous scheduld 4 demolishyun on 5th
ave off th cornr uv yew n 5th in kitsilano n i saw th landlord we
had just cum back from mexico n nevada wher we had got in2
sum trubuls n also had remarkabul n soaring times i think may
b we wer renting ther 4 sum fortee dollars a month ths was may
b 1965 we wer all still starting beginning our lives in art n in life
n thees wer xhilerating times 4 manee uv us n we wer working
against th war in vietnam manee uv us in vancouvr trying 2 stop
that amerikan imperialist war

sum uv th floor bords wer missing in sum places in th hous n th
heeting system was spottee th basement furnace tuk sawdust
we wer printing books thru our press blewointmentpress milton
acorn was booking me in2 dewing poetree reedings he wud put
2gethr in th meeting n prforming hall bhind n part uv vanguard
books on granville st th hedquartrs uv th leeg 4 soshulist acksyun
thees reedings wer reelee well attendid freqwentlee present ther
n reeding wer pat lowther maxine gadd maxine n pat both alwayze
amayzing writrs milton acorn brillyant writr n othrs martina
clinton nevr wantid 2 reed out lowd but she was a brillyant writr

sew milton bgan 2 visit us in our hous on 5th as he had alredee
visitid us in our hous on fleming b4 we wer encouragd 2 leev town

n go 2 nevada n mexico on fleming st he bout from me th first
painting i evr sold n we wud talk whil we wer getting dinnr redee
with his cigars going saying "i shout love" leev by th back door n
go around 2 th front door n re-entr thru th front door still talking
declaiming n still smoking all ths was sew reelee wundrful n in th
old brown hous on 5th he talkd abt us dewing a book 2gethr n in
th back uv anothr brokn down hous next door ther was an old room
wch we usd 2 write ' i want to tell you love' wch was his idea n i
grew quiklee 2 love it

2 peopul with similar beleefs yet veree diffrent poetree
approaches in th same book a veree radikul idea as it
turnd out evreewher we wer in thees buildings th floor
bords wer unevn n cud spring up at yu we wer working
on our book me audishyuning pomes 2 milton n we pulld
it 2gethr as yu c heer n nowun wantid it our approaches
n styles 2 diffrent from each othr they wud all say n that
was uv kours th point uv our book

going 2 c raymond souster

manee yeers latr eric schmaltz n i met on yonge st n went
2 c dr marsee at her brillyant fresh cookd great food countr
in th back uv pusateris on church that was xcelent n thn we
went 2 th bloor line going west 2 wher raymond livd neer high
park that was oct 17 2012 that was 2 dayze b4 raymond went
2 spirit he was veree affabul n genuinlee pleezd 2 c us
he playd johnny hartman 4 us a beautiful vois n sum xcelent
dixie gave us each his nu book he was in a lovlee place a big
living room n a bedroom n a bath room he n his wife living
 in th same building uv assistid living wud visit each othr n hang
evree day with each othr

raymond rememberd milton acorn sew well he told us they had
servd in world war 2 2gethr eric had bin resurfacing i want to

tell you love th book i wrote with milton acorn in th mid sixteez
i sd 2 raymond n nowun wud publish as our writing approaches
wer sew diffrent peopul sd we cudint b in th same book that
was th point milton n i wud say 2 peopul sheesh but xcelens
can happn ths manee yeers latr eric wanting th book 2 happn
milton n me workd sew hard on we wer sew deeplee in2 th
choices wch pomes wher how they wud enhans each othr

whn we wer both with raymond eric n me raymond sd he lovd
milton as did i   raymond sd he didint reelee know abt our
book but his memoreez uv milton acorn wer veree vivid n he
enjoyd talking abt him how they each had chosn diffrent life
paths evenshulee as raymond n i also had dun his chois a
mor guaranteed path with benefits such as a gud pensyun from
bank work sew he cud live ther wher he was

n milton n myself much mor precarious paths but who
is 2 say wch is bettr reelee raymond softlee n beautifulee
sd it was wundrful 2 meet him aftr such a long time whn
i had met him wuns b4 at a literaree partee at gerry n
arlenes place also in toronto prhaps ovr 40 yeers ago
but i dont know sew much whn things happn i seem
like manee poets 2 live in sum continuing present

whn we left raymond we each huggd him veree warmlee
n him each uv us he seemd veree fit it was xciting 2
spend ovr an hour wundrful qualitee time with raymond
both eric n i wer startuld that 2 dayze latr raymond souster
went 2 spirit leeving sew manee frends n lives n memoreez
i was reelee hopeing 2 c him agen n talk n listn 2 jazz
mewsik with him agen

saturday march 16 2019 beautiful snow fall huge soft
flakes rolling thru th air walking down th street tord
wher th street car stops n goez on furthr west n getting

off on spadina crossing spadina 2 walk south 2 baldwin
wher th secret hand shake club hous n art galleree
is i notisd first time th waverly hotel was gone wher
milton acorn livd b4 n aftr vancouvr b4 he returnd 2
prins edward island wher he went 2 spirit august 20 1986
      if now ths manee yeers n mor 4 milton acorn 2 still
      " ...want to tell us love.."

dissimilar apertures uv consciousness: An Interview with bill bissett

This conversation between bill bissett and Eric Schmaltz was conducted over email from April 14, 2011 until May 28, 2011, and was first published in *Open Letter* 15, No. 1 (Fall 2012): pp. 58-63.

Eric Schmaltz: bill, I understand that sometime in the early 1960s you began working on a manuscript with the iconic and influential Milton Acorn in Vancouver, British Columbia. Acorn had already published several books while you were just beginning your career as a poet. This manuscript, entitled *I Want to Tell you Love*, was completed, but never published. Sadly, since then, it has almost entirely been out of the public eye. The story behind *I Want to Tell You Love* and your collaboration with Milton Acorn is what I would like to talk to you about. Could you tell me about how you and Milton Acorn first met?

bill bissett: i first met milton acorn at th vanguard books th bookstore 4 th leeg uv soshulist acksyun in vancouvr on granville st neer th granvile st bridg

a wundrful prson ther   ruth bullock introdusd us i think i was with lance farrell at th time 2 milton acorn he had built all th shelving ther 4 th bookstore   he was a great carpentr n a great poet i liked him veree much n cud reelee groov with him get in synch with him   i arrivd in van summer 58   it was th day th second narrows bridg being built collapsd ther wer fataliteez milton n i startid working on i want 2 tell yu love in 65 whn me n my family i was part uv livd veree cheeplee in a hous that was being torn down   martina clinton n me n our dottr michelle it was aftr we returnd from an amayzing journee thru california nevada arizona mexico n back   our dottr was still veree young maybe 4 yeers its strange abt dates isint it how we can want xaktitude as gertrude stein sd xaktitude as kings n yet ther is a strangelee elusiv qualitee abt it all wch is uv kours what she was implying   milton n me wud talk 4 hours n hours n walk n talk n talk n walk my first evr painting sale was 2 him   that was sew amayzing n thru our talking th idea uv our dewing a book 2gethr was n did evolv sew wundrfulee   milton had sent it 2 raymound souster n othrs it was continualee being turnd down bcoz it was sd our styles wer 2 dissimilar well that was our point diffrent approaches cud well b in th same book sew its xciting 4 me that its being lookd at now whn th vanguard books meeting tuk place ium not sure that was th first meeting btween me n milton   i think it was whn we rtnd from mexico thos dates 65ish   maybe n milton startid an amayzing reeding sereez in th back uv th vanguard book store   with him me pat lane pat lowthr maxine gadd   judith copithorne n othrs it was a wundrful brillyant venu   beth jankola that was an amayzing sereez milton wud introduce each uv us n oftn b smoking his belovd cigar it was a wundrful erlee xperiens

Eric Schmaltz: Acorn was known for his community-building efforts. He provided forums for people to voice their opinions on anything, especially poetry and politics. Acorn helped many young poets this way. I have read that Acorn might have organized your first poetry reading. Perhaps you can tell me a little bit about your first reading experience?

bill bissett: my first reeding was akshulee at th cellar jazz club in vankouvr in watson ave   i was using manee voices in my reedings thn   not content with onlee wun voice i reelee wantid 2 xplorr manee voices   peopul didint like what i was dewing n threw stuff at me xcellent   thers a pome abt ths reeding in th

book sailor from talonbooks also jamie reid wrote abt that nite at th cellar my first reeding
milton acorns sereez uv reedings at th beautiful hall in th vanguard books was i think th first sereez iud evr bin part uv n miltons organizing n emseeing was wundrful kind n veree supportiv uv all uv us me pat lane maxine gadd pat lowthr beth jankola judith copithorne it was eklektik all pushing diffrent boundareez uv stylee n consciousness tho we all promotid soshul consern n workd against th war in vietnam i was finding a much mor singul vois thn n an xtensyun uv my speaking vois th drama uv manee voices wch i dew a littul bit agen latr n continuing was put aside sum 2 discovr n show a vois uv soshul caring love n dissolusyun reelee certinlee criteeking uv th warring klass strugguls n such systems within a countree within canada e g th pome th canadian killer whale n th body all uv wch ar in beyond evn faithful legends being part uv ths sereez uv miltons at th vanguard books was a veree important part uv th road uv my poetree development 4 me

Eric Schmaltz: How would you describe *I Want to Tell You Love*?

bill bissett: a book uv poetree by 2 poets diffrent n similar like gertrude stein sd evreething is a book uv poetree by 2 peopul uv simultaneouslee similar n dissimilar apertures uv consciousness cultural n psychik leenings urges phraseolojees uv lettrs tropes beerings weight uv n breks uv th lines getting 2gethr using conversaysyunal n xplorativ xperimental n mor normativ n poetik fixtures uv langwage arts living th dreem diffrentlee xpressd uv kours n sharing th devosyun practise n loving beem being aware n unkonscious sew 2 make art art that speeks loudlee n whispring intonaysyuns 2 our selvs remedee n 2 othrs i want 2 tell yu love

Eric Schmaltz: You mentioned earlier that the idea for *I Want to Tell You Love* arose from your conversations with Milton. What sorts of things were the two of you talking about? How did these conversations inspire or influence your decision to collaborate on a book of poetry?

bill bissett: milton n i reelee beleevd that love reseeving it xtending it feeling it was always reelee ther was at th heart uv evreething n we wantid our book 2 show that th brekdown uv sew manee taboos n bcumming kleer 2gethr   all peopul cud subdue th war impulses in our specees   that beleef cud b a big leep n sew on it was howevr what we wer reelee wrestuling with n xtoling   4 all its still apparent pitfalls mor abt ths bit latr tho ok ium travelling in a few minits n i want 2 rtn 2 ths thred...
...returning 2 th continuing thred uv how we can apply love in sew manee situaysyuns that in itself th praxis uv being n espeshulee 2 diffrent approaches within th same book confirms n spreds that releesing from th hegemonee uniformitee wun message or approach pr book or uniformitee thruout evn parts uv th book thematisizing evree breth n wind shield n beep we wantid th manee n mor n love imbued 2 heel n salv solv th hurts n burdns we wer n ar still n mooving beleeving all that i think ther sew espeshulee uv miltons pome 2 sydney anne i want to tell you love was reelee a labour uv love in all its parts whats handid down 2 us sorting that n carreeing on with nu nu moments nu lives   n th beleef that if peopul love n feel love they dont hurt ths view takes sum heet on th world weeree stage we wer ar up 4 that knowing admitting that thats a continuin kleering letting go within ourselvs as well   it dusint stop ther is no stopping we ar th nite we ar alwayze moving in2 n we want 2 tell yu love
collaboraysyun sew interesting sum peopul with whom th work i dew mite have sum strong similariteez   othrs with whom th approach may look n b reelee veree different may b abul 2 collaborate on othr issews n veree deeplee milton n me wer in2 just that reelee   politikalee we wer veree similar we wer in2 guaranteeing th freedom n life comforts 4 evreewun we wer n

still ar veree egalitarian we didint like class war we wer n still ar apalld that sum view th class war as inevitabul that its sum kind uv darwinian drama 2 b admird we did not beleev in anee divine rites uv kings or qweens n that th ruling elite n all its mystifkaysuns n justifikaysyuns practisd as entitulment th terribul tyranee uv th most absurd cruel punishments we both beleevd that it is not writtn aneewher that sum peopul shud have less or way less thn othrs 2day milton acorn wud b enraged that in th yewnitid states 1% uv th peopul own n control ovr 60% uv that countreez wealth canada is bettr from an egalitarian equalizasyun point uv view but not much bettr evreething can b trackd now norway has th leest gap btween rich n th othrs we wud talk abt thees things 4 hours he sporadikalee leeving th place we wud b in n returning via th back door if he had left by th front during our talk his cigar smoke sew constantlee reeling around his hed n koffing as he returnd inside continuing a brillyant point he wud b making

Eric Schmaltz: Milton Acorn's "Poem for Sydney" reflects some of the core themes that are present in the manuscript. It speaks to the idea of humanity's interconnectedness that comes out in a number of both of your poems. You mentioned that *I Want to Tell You Love* attempts "2 show that th brekdown uv sew manee taboos n bcumming kleer 2gethr." What were the specific taboos you and Acorn were responding to at the time?

bill bissett: oh sew manee taboos against aborsyun gay love sheltrs 4 homeless peopul repressive laws against marijuana whn alcohol was sew encouragd taboos against peopul wanting 2 n protesting against th war in Vietnam politikul writing all these n mor

Eric Schmaltz: I am beginning to see that *I Want to Tell You Love* was written as a response to issues that you and Acorn cared deeply about. This is not a surprise to me. I know Acorn began a group called "Artists Against Vietnam" as an effort to protest the war. "Artists Against Vietnam" was among the many efforts Acorn made to encourage people to unite, talk about issues, and get involved. The 'Thursday night blab sessions' at the Advance Mattress Coffee House is another example of Acorn's efforts. A "blab session" was supposedly a place where people would congregate to talk about anything that they cared about. Conversation seems to have been an important part of Acorn's work. You mentioned that *I Want to Tell You Love* emerged from your own talks with Acorn. Were there ever issues you and Acorn disagreed on?

bill bissett: no

Eric Schmaltz: In the context of the manuscript "love" functions in a variety of ways. It speaks to ideas of healing as well as interconnectedness. I am also getting the sense that you and Acorn thought/think "love" was/is the solution to the political and social issues you mentioned before. Is that correct? Could you perhaps elaborate on what "love" might have meant to you and Acorn and how it might relate to some specific issues you mentioned?

bill bissett: we wer n ar alwayze beleevin that remembring 2 feel loving as much as possibul we all carree baggage n 2 b aktivlee within wunself involvd in letting all that go processing enuff 2 keep on feeling loving n ther4 undew all th warrings

Eric Schmaltz: One of the main criticisms of the manuscript was the multiple, opposing voices present. Your poetic voice and Acorn's poetic voice are obviously very different. This seeming opposition was one of the reasons why the manuscript was never published. Did you see your voices as opposing?

bill bissett: i gess what we ar all beginning 2 accept n realize is that diffrens is not opposisyun
diffrens is enhansing can b   evree brain is diffrent n uv kours that was veree much th space we wer cumming from n   we did talk a lot abt   supporting multipul voices 2gethr on long walks n inside th hous we wer veree much disappointid n

opposd 2 th cultur uv sameness that was encroaching n trying 2 dominate peopuls lives

Eric Schmaltz: The two of you tried a number of times to get the manuscript published, but no one would take it. Why didn't the two of you attempt to self-publish or even later publish it with blewointment?

bill bissett: thats a great qwestyun i dont know i dont remembr i think i wantid 2 with blewointment n sum things stood in th way at that time it was a big book fr sure blewointment was veree limitid at that time why not latr whn blewintment bcame less limitid i dont reelee remember what th obstakuls or th discouragmnent issews wer life moovd veree fast thn but maybe its getting publishd now or soon

Eric Schmaltz: For the most part, the manuscript appears to be written separately. Your poems and Acorn's poems are interspersed. In what ways did the two of you write this together?

bill bissett: We wer working 2gethr 4 th vishyun uv disparate voices beings working 2gethr we wud suggest n work 4 inklewsyu uv each othrs pomes that wud dew that evn tho each uv our pomes wer uv kours writtn separatelee

Eric Schmaltz: In what way do you think *I Want to Tell You Love* is a collaboration?

bill bissett: we made it 2gethr put it 2gethr talkd 4 hours wch pome wher all that

Eric Schmaltz: How did collaborating with Acorn differ from your other collaborative efforts?

bill bissett: ium reelee xcitid 2 think abt sew manee peopul iuv workd with n continu 2 dew sew   helene ducharme dewing sound poetree with her shes an opera singr n with honey novick with whom iuv dun mor thn elevn reedings uv th embrace sound pome shes a wundrful singr as well as a wundrful poet th embrace sound pome its 20 minits from th book time in durham st catharines n at nac in st catharines wher as yu know th embrace booth was showing 4 sum months jordan stones filming uv th stills uv my paintings shot by mark belvedere n with th mewsik uv bowen mcconnie n with sum uv th vizual ovr lays by shane nagel in a continuous loop n in toronto sew manee places hamilton galiano island gabriola island 4 whom undr ths aegis uv hilary peach th embrace pome was first creatid iuv sumtimes dun it on my own gabriola island othr places with th moovee jordan stone made uv my paintings th stills uv wch shot by mark belvedere n th music uv bowen mcconnie thees last few yeers have bin wunderful 4 me working n playing with thees n othr peopul   it is wunderful 2 dew things with othr peopul now ium on a tour uv europe with adeena karasick dewing reedings 2gethr in england france spain belgium switzerland n russia ths is veree collaborativ as well wch like thees othr projekts cudint work if we didint work 2gethr we n all thees peopul mensyund heer work veree well 2gethr mostlee iuv collaboratid with musicians composrs othr sound poets ths was diffrent bcoz it embodeed diffrens in an overt way 2 reelee diffrrent writrs within th same book

Eric Schmaltz: Shortly after meeting, you and Acorn became good friends. I get a sense that Acorn also served as a mentor to you. Would you describe your relationship in this way? What did you learn from Acorn about writing and poetry?

bill bissett: i reelee lernd from milton 2 get it out ther milton acorn was definitlee a mentor 2 me he bought a painting from me th first art sale i evr made he prsuadid canadian forum 2 print a pome uv mine calld th body n was th first pome uv mine evr publishd he was definitlee a mentor 2 me frend n guide

Eric Schmaltz: Lastly, the title of the manuscript is curious. It is written in the singular voice even though there are two authors and two voices (at least). Why did you and Acorn choose the singular instead of the plural? Why not "We want to tell you love"?

bill bissett: its less uv a teem as th we sumtimes can b we each wantid 2 say 2 stand in 4 evree "i" a plea from evreewun

TH
CARUSO
POME[1]

       writtn in tandem with the great
       caruso screenplay whil watching
       th film writing in th dark lines from
       th skript n from my viewr mind a
       form uv found pome in homage 2
          th brillyant n epik ekonomee uv
          th skript uv sonia levien
            n william ludwig

we have calld

    so much

        sentimental

that we have

    very little

left

   prhaps nothing

---

[1] This edition of *I Want to Tell You Love* contains "The Caruso Poem" as it first appeared in the 1965 typescript. This is a revised version of "The Caruso Poem" by bissett, which reveals that this poem corresponds to the found poetry tradition. Readers can see which words and phrases are bissett's and which are drawn from the 1951 film *The Great Caruso*, as indicated by bissett's italics. bissett recognizes this later version to be the real, intended version of the poem.

CARUSO

you have a voice
    the galleries go clear
to the sky

you must use it
his mother found
it appropriate
to entomb the needs
of one's particular
self in order to give
to others what
    God has bestowed

*it is enough for th
rest of the world / it
is enough for here*

    *this time my
frends
i must be alone*

**listen closely
to the dialogue / you
will know an aspect
of what is**

i do not sing
in america

he will sing
for an emergency

most of the people
sit in the galleries

    sing to them
i am a peasant
he is gentle

    snuff to
clear the head

whiskey to clear the throat
watr to wash
  down the whiskey

    curtains
mr. Caruso

/ sorry father i was
thinking

we are glad
 to see
each other
  here

up in the galleries
they know this man
    he keeps
      his hands
    in his pockets

          (we talkd
of an electric storm and it came
: there is foreshadowing

 and the vein
of success
 running through it

one who knows
  cheers
now they will all clap

you were
wonderful
mr. caruso

  in the excitement
  i lost my glove

    i sing

   i am a peasant
        standing
      in a carriage
      dressd
      in fur and blue
      velvet

PLEASE
DON'T
FORGET   (ME)

   i sing / the sentry
  with the spear
  paces on top
  of the fortifications

            mr. caruso
            ium from th Globe

its my furst
assignment
you promised me

DO YOU LOVE ME
I THINK I FELL
IN LOVE WITH YOU
THE FIRST
TIME I HEARD
YOU SING

you sing
yes but can you
carry a spear

i carried sacks
of flour

can she
give her life
to his voice

artists of the metropolitan
sing for the liberty
loan fund

enrico
   you promised

  the truth is
  the man does not
  have the voice
   the voice has him

       a sense
  of the fitness of things

      back to the choir
where mother told him
      to sing for God

  ava maria
  candles arch ways
  all
  reaches
  upward

      (they
             elope

and are later
photographed
walkng in the
easter
parade

    words fall
    into rhyme

we can skip
       over
 some of it / he
simply
  gave

    his daughter
    born / everyone
    glad to see
    each othur
    there

    her father
    with held his
    blessings
    to believe
     in foreshadowing
    they called
    his daughter
    gloria

    underneath it
  all   he lost
   his voice

   and hid
   his despair

to relax
the throat
he uses ether

soon they began
to wish that he wud
not sing / his voice

was
  everyone's

how long can you
  sing on ether

why did he lose
his voice he wudint
see a doctor

    curtains
    senor Caruso

because she wudint
let him

because he resented
his mother

because she had
to practice to sing

because her father
with held his blessing

because of
  the candles is
that it
  that no
  one voice
  can sing
    forever

    th myth
     has him
    die
        when his voice
       dies
       and that
       is the end

    sonya levien was wun uv th most prolifik n
sought aftr hollywood screen writers uv
th 1920s 30s 40s n th 50s
with william ludwig a few times co-writr she
reseevd th oscar 4 best screen writing 4
    "interrupted melody" in 1955
    she n they reseevd othr veree worthee
    nominaysyuns
    sonya levien livd an xtraordinaree life n
    career (1888-1960)

    all th lines in italiks ar from th skript uv
    th great caruso by sonya levien n william
    ludwig

Editorial Rationale

I Want to Tell You Love was never published in its intended form as a collaborative book. Three typescripts of the collection exist—one is located in Milton Acorn's fond at Library and Archives Canada (LAC) in Ottawa and the other two are held in bill bissett's fond at the Clara Thomas Special Collections at York University in Toronto. Each of these copies is nearly identical in form and content, despite some minor handwritten corrections across the three versions.

While this collection is not a true facsimile of the typescripts, in preparing this book for publication the editorial rationale maintains close fidelity to the original typescripts.

Despite this rationale, some minor alterations to its material appearance and construction were necessary. Beginning with the cover, we used the original, intended cover image for the collection, while adding our names as editors to acknowledge our labour in the process of publication. This cover image has been digitally scanned and reproduced. Additionally, the original cover image and all pages of the book were typewritten onto 8.5 by 11-inch sheets and staple bound. In transforming *I Want to Tell You Love* from typescript to publication, the size of the book has been altered to appear in a poetry book size familiar to today's poetry reading audience.

For the text of the poems themselves, the editors were faithful to the typescripts in almost every instance. The text has been transcribed from the original manuscript into a digital form, including minor handwritten corrections that were made to a small number of poems, presumably by the authors since they appear across two of the three existing copies of the typescript. In selecting our source text, we opted to transcribe the LAC's version of the typescript since it is the most complete version of the manuscript. One version of the manuscript in the Clara Thomas Special Collections is missing, for example, bissett's "The Tucson Owls," which has been mysteriously (likely mistakenly) ripped out. That same poem, however, appears in the LAC version and a second version at the Clara Thomas. We have retained all stylistic conventions found in the typescript, including punctuation and spelling. Editorial intervention in the text was limited to correcting only the most obvious typos or errors, which are listed in the "Editors' Emendations." In the cases where titles were not attributed to poems, we opted to use "Untitled" in place of an official title. We have also not altered the poem order of the manuscript. The poems appear in this edition in the same order they appear in the copytext. All images have been digitally scanned and reproduced.

Many of the poems that appear inside *I Want to Tell You Love* also appear in other, separately authored publications, including later collected and selected works. Most of these later publications include slight changes or edits to the poems. However, these publications occurred after the typescript was created, and as a result, the editors have decided not to include the edits to the text. Instead, in "Emendations as Presented in Later Published Poems" of this edition, we have provided a list of all the emendations between the text as printed here, and the versions of the poems printed in the authors' major publications.

Explanatory Notes

These explanatory notes are intended to clarify many of the various historical references and some of the terms that appear in *I Want to Tell You Love*. Within reason, these notes specifically focus on identifying the locations and historical figures mentioned in the poems, both actual and mythological. All persons and places that could be identified with some degree of certainty were listed and the rest were omitted.

"Crossing Directions" by bill bissett
1. "the Metaphysical poets were, Marvell" (Part 2, Line 3) — Reference to Andrew Marvell (1621-1678), the English Metaphysical poet who was known for poems such as "To His Coy Mistress."
2. "This summer evening, our daughter" (Part 2, Line 6) — Reference to Ooljah Bissett (1962-2012), who later changed her name to Michelle Bissett.

"Poem" ["Hair flowing yellow and still"] by Milton Acorn
1. "I / saw my sister once" (Lines 2-3) — Acorn, the oldest of five children, had three sisters: Katherine, Mary, and Helen.

"The Slaughter of Innocents" by Milton Acorn
1. The title of the poem is likely a reference to the biblical narrative known as "The Massacre of the

Innocents" in the New Testament (Gospel of Matthew 2: 16-18) in which Herod orders the execution of all male children two years old and under in the vicinity of Bethlehem.
2. Fetlock (line 2) — A joint in a horse's foot.

"Spartacus" by Milton Acorn
1. Spartacus (c. 111–71 BC) was a gladiator known for leading a major slave uprising against the Roman Republic.

"a carriage that were green" by bill bissett
1. "the houses / on our street" (Lines 3-4) — bissett and Martina Clinton lived near the corner of Yew Street and 5th Avenue, in Kitsilano in Vancouver, British Columbia.

"from five poems for norman mailer" by bill bissett
1. The title references Norman Mailer (1923-2007), the influential American novelist journalist, essayist, playwright, film-maker, actor, and socialist activist. By the mid-1960s, Mailer had published numerous works of fiction such as *The Naked and the Dead* (1948) and *Deer Park* (1955) as well as essays, such as the controversial "The White Negro" (1957).

"Poem for Sydney" by Milton Acorn
1. The title references Sydney Anne, a club singer in Vancouver who would sing at venues such as The Flat Five, where bissett also read poetry.

"The Body" by bill bissett
1. "So we rode far out to strawberry island" (Line 4) — Likely a reference to Strawberry Island, Tofino, British Columbia.

"Poem for a Singer" by Milton Acorn
1. "throbbing thru that figurehead / to the heroic Argo" (Lines 6-7) — Argo was mythological Greek hero Jason, leader of the Argonauts, a band of heroes.
2. "No Gods / they have but gray abstractions mulling / in the flaccid null-brain of Moloch" (Lines 33-35) — Moloch, the biblical name of a Canaanite God associated with child sacrifice.

"there is the voodoo in the town" by bill bissett
1. "R C M P" (Line 5) — Royal Canadian Mounted Police
2. "goya had a message the queen got it queen elizabeth london looked" (Line 10) — Here, bissett references the Spanish Romantic painter Francisco Goya (1746-1828). bissett also references "queen elizabeth london," Queen Elizabeth II (1926-Present), Queen of the United Kingdom and the Commonwealth.
3. "at a Goya / painting of a spaniard" (Line 10-11) — This is likely a reference to Goya's famous painting *The Third of May 1808* (1814), which commemorates the Spanish resistance to Napoleon's armies during the occupation of 1808 in the Peninsular War. Admittedly, some of the figures in Goya's painting do

appear to have haircuts that resemble the rock band The Beatles famous haircuts known as the mop-top.
   4. "gerald kelly" (Line 11) — Sir Gerald Kelly (1879-1972), a British painter who was President of the Royal Academy from 1949 until 1954.

"News in a Letter" by Milton Acorn
   1. "My brother's bought an organ" (Line 1) — Acorn's younger brother's name is Robert.
   2. "Tiger Rag" (Line 9) — A Jazz standard recorded and released in 1917 by the Original Dixieland Jass Band (Eddie Edwards, Nick LaRocca, Henry Ragas, Tony Sbarbaro, and Larry Shields). It is one of the most commonly recorded Jazz songs.

"we sleep inside each other all" by bill bissett
   1. "date square" (Line 30) — a Canadian dessert made of cooked dates with an oatmeal crumb topping.

"Poem" ["You'll climb or fall from this moment"] by Milton Acorn
   1. Cairn (Line 11) — A manmade pile of stones, used for a number of purposes, including landmarks, burial monuments, and other ceremonial purposes.

"for Martina" by bill bissett
   1. Prior to meeting Acorn, and sometime around 1965, bissett, Clinton, and their daughter, Michelle, travelled through the United States in California, Nevada, Arizona, and then Mexico. bissett makes reference to this trip in the interview, "dissimilar apertures uv consciousness: An Interview with bill bissett," in this edition.

2. "Nogales" (Line 1) — Nogales is a city in Santa Cruz County, Arizona.

3. "Tepic" (Line 1) — Tepic is the capital and largest city of the western Mexican state of Nayarit.

4. "Mazatlan" (Line 2) — Mazatlán is a city in the Mexican state of Sinaloa.

5. "Guadalajara" (Line 2) — Guadalajara is a metropolis in western Mexico and the capital of the state of Jalisco.

6. "Tlaquepaque" (Line 4) — Tlaquepaque, historically known as San Pedro Tlaquepaque, is a city and the surrounding municipality in the Mexican state of Jalisco.

7. "Ajijic" (Line 4) — Ajijic is a town part of the municipality also called Chapala, in the State of Jalisco, Mexico.

8. "Chapala" (Line 5) — Chapala is a town and municipality in the central Mexican state of Jalisco.

9. "Morelia" (Line 5) — Morelia is a city and municipality in the state of Michoacán in central Mexico.

10. "Michoacan" (Line 6) — Michoacán, officially known as Estado Libre y Soberano de Michoacán de Ocampo, is one state of the Federal Entities of Mexico.

11. "Ciudad de Mexico" (Line 7) — Translates from Spanish to Mexico City, which is the capital city and largest city of Mexico.

12. "Acapulco" (Line 10) — Formally known as Acapulco de Juárez, a city, municipality and major seaport in the state of Guerrero.

13. "Zihuatanejo" (Line 10) — Zihuatanejo is the fourth-largest city in the Mexican state of Guerrero.
14. "La Barrita" (Line 11) — Fishing and beach area in Petatlán in the state of Guerrero in Mexico.
15. "Cayacal" (Line 11) — Island in Lázaro Cárdenas, Mexico.
16. "Chilipancingo" (Line 13) — Chilpancingo de los Bravo is the capital and second-largest city of the state of Guerrero, Mexico.
17. "Taxco" (Line 13) — Taxco de Alarcón is a small city located in state of Guerrero, Mexico.
18. "Cuernavaca" (Line 14) — Cuernavaca is the capital and largest city of the state of Morelos in Mexico.
19. "San / Jeronimo" (Line 14-15) — San Jerónimo Lídice is a former village, now part of Mexico City.

"Two Visions" by Milton Acorn
1. "ten-pins" (Line 4) — bowling pins.

"Las Palmas" by bill bissett
1. The title of the poem likely refers to the town of Valle de las Palmas in the Municipality of Tecate (in the State of Baja California).
2. "La Barrita" (Line 10) — see note about La Barrita above.

"whilst waiting for" by bill bissett
1. "peter lorre and / Vincent / price" (Line 2-4) — Peter Lorre (1904-1964) was a popular film star in the 1940s, often starring alongside Humphrey Bogart, and appeared in popular films such as *The Maltese*

Falcon. Vincent Price (1911-1993) was Vincent Leonard Price Jr., another popular American actor best known for his performances in films, including *House of Wax* (1953), *House on Haunted Hill* (1959), and *The Last Man on Earth* (1964). In the early 1960s, Lorre and Price co-starred in several horror movies, such as *The Comedy of Terrors* (1963) and *The Raven* (1963).

"One Day Kennedy Died and So Did the Birdman of Alcatraz" by Milton Acorn
1. The title of the poem makes reference to John F. Kennedy (1917-1963), who was the 35th president of the United States from January 1961 until his assassination in November 1963, and Robert Franklin Stroud (1890-1963), also known as the "Birdman of Alcatraz," who was a convicted murderer imprisoned in the maximum security prison, known as Alcatraz, in San Francisco, California, United States of America. They died in 1963 within one day of each other.
2. "Prince Charley" (Line 16) — Charles, Prince of Wales (b. 1948) is heir to the British Throne as the eldest son of Queen Elizabeth II.
3. "Churchill's Cigar" (Line 19) — Sir Winston Leonard Spencer-Churchill (1874-1965) was Prime Minister of the United Kingdom from 1940-1945 and then again from 1951-1955. Churchill's image was defined by his habit for smoking cigars.
4. "Krushchev's shoe" (Line 19) — Nikita Sergeyevich Khrushchev (1894-1971) was First Secretary of the Communist Party of the Soviet Union from 1953 until 1964. On 12 October 1960, Krushchev

heightened his notoriety when he reportedly pulled off his shoe and banged it on his desk during a United Nations debate.

5. "Sartre" (Line 32) — Jean-Paul Sartre (1905-1980), the French philosopher, playwright, novelist, screenwriter, political activist, biographer, literary critic, and Nobel Prize winner for Literature, who is known for his contributions to existentialism and phenomenology.

"song of a virgins" by bill bissett

1. "navaho" (Line 13) — British English spelling of Navajo, a Native American people of the Southwestern United States.

2. "damascus" (Line 22) — The capital city of Syria.

"Headlights" by bill bissett

1. "Singa" (Part 2, Line 8) — a figure from the mythology of the Batak people of Indonesia. Described as part human, part water buffalo, and part crocodile, it represents a benevolent and protective power.

2. "Joyce" (Part 2, Line 9) — James Joyce (1882-1941), the famous Irish novelist known for *A Portrait of the Artist as a Young Man* (1916) and *Ulysses* (1922), among other works.

3. "Chilipancingo" (Part 3, Line 3) — see note above re: Chilipancingo.

4. "Los Charros" (Part 3, Line 4) — Charros are traditional horsemen from Mexico.

5. "Picadors" (Part 3, Line 4) — Spanish-styled bullfighters. A picador is a lancer mounted on

horseback who assists a matador, who is the person trying to kill the bull in a bullfight.
6. "gorging / on Eskimales" (Part 3, Line 7-8) — Likely a reference to "esquimales," ice pops coated in chocolate and confections.

"The Man in the Iron Mask" by Milton Acorn
1. The title of the poem refers to the much mythologized, unidentified prisoner who was arrested in 1669 or 1670 and subsequently held in a number of French prisons. His face was always covered by a mask of black velvet cloth.

"suite of five" by bill bissett
1. "spring days, schubert / string quartets" (Part 1, Lines 1-2) — Franz Schubert (1797-1828), an Austrian composer of the late Classical and early Romantic eras.
2. "a / color only Van Gogh had" (Part 5, Lines 6-7) — Vincent Van Gogh (1853-1890), an influential Dutch post-impressionist painter.

Poem ["My mother goes in slippers"] by Milton Acorn
1. "My mother goes in slippers" (Line 1) — Milton Acorn's mother, Helen Acorn (later Helen Jewel).

"Khrushchev's Shoe" by Milton Acorn
1. See reference above regarding "Krushchev's shoe" in "One Day Kennedy Died and So Did the Birdman of Alcatraz."

"As I Think of Where Today I can Get th Rent Money" by bill bissett

1. "There's two wars on, / both run by the U.S., one in Vietnam, th other / in Dominican Republic" (Lines 3-6) — The Vietnam War was a significant conflict in Vietnam, Laos, and Cambodia from 1 November 1955 to the fall of Saigon on 30 April 1975. It was officially fought by North Vietnam and South Vietnam, with significant support given to South Vietnam by the United States of America, while the Soviet Union and China supported North Vietnam. Some consider it a Cold War proxy war. The Dominican Civil War took place between 24 April 1965, and 3 September 1965, in Santo Domingo, Dominican Republic. In late April, during this conflict, the United States military intervened into the conflict.

"The Fountain" by bill bissett

1. "Hiroshima, Dresden" (Line 55) — Hiroshima, a city in Japan. Dresden, a city in Germany. Both were significantly damaged by allied bombings during the Second World War. The attack on Hiroshima was the first time an atomic bomb had been used in warfare, destroying the city and forfetting Japan's surrender. It showed the world what the devastation of a nuclear war would look like.

2. "Dachau" (Line 59) — Dachau was the first of the Nazi concentration camps opened in 1933.

3. "Skid Row" (Line 62) — Skid Row is a neighbourhood in Los Angeles, California. It is known for its large homeless population.

4. "General / Motors, M.G.M., NATO" (Line 98-99) — General Motors, multinational corporation headquartered in Detroit that designs, manufactures, markets, and distributes vehicles and vehicle parts. MGM, also known as Metro-Goldwyn-Mayer, is an American media company. NATO, also known as the North Atlantic Treaty Organization, is an intergovernmental security alliance between thirty North American and European countries.
5. "Raphael" (Line 126) — Likely a reference to Italian Renaissance painter Raffaello Sanzio da Urbino (1483-1520).

"Death Poem" by Milton Acorn
1. "Marilyn's death" (Line 9) — Reference to Marilyn Monroe (1926-1962), the famous and beloved American actress and model. One of the most popular sex symbols of the fifties and sixties, she remains a pop culture icon. Monroe's suicide on 4 August 1962 was front-page news around the world.

"The Tucson Owls" by bill bissett
1. The title of the poem refers to the city of Tucson, Arizona.
2. "Malcolm X" (Line 11) — Malcolm X (1925-1965), also known as El-Hajj Malik El-Shabazz, was a well-known American Muslim minister and human rights activist who was a popular figure during the Civil Rights movement. One of the most influential African Americans in history, he was assassinated on 21 February 1965.

3. "Lincoln" (Line 21) — A luxury motor vehicle produced by Lincoln, formally the Lincoln Motor Company.
4. "the owl of minerva" (Line 24) — In Latin myth, the Owl of Minerva typically represents Minerva, the Roman goddess of wisdom and strategic warfare.
5. "George Washington's birthday" (Line 26) — George Washington was born on 22 February 1732.
6. "Salmo at the Cranbrook- / Creston cut-off" (Lines 29-30) — Salmo is a village in the West Kootenay region of southeastern British Columbia, Canada. Creston is a nearby small town and Cranbrook a small city.
7. "There had been a copy of Harlow by the bed" (Line 52) — Likely a reference to *Harlow: An Intimate Biography* by Irving Shulman published in 1964. It is the biography of Jean Harlow, one of the most popular American actresses and sex symbols of the 1930s.
8. "Castlegar" (Line 59) — Castlegar is a city in the West Kootenay region of British Columbia.

"Detail of a Cityscape" by Milton Acorn
1. "cripple" (Line 2) — A now offensive term used to refer to a person with a physical disability. At the time, it was commonplace.

"Does the Negro's Soft Voice" by Milton Acorn
1. The title uses the controversial word "negro," a term historically used to denote persons of Black African heritage. It was once considered a polite term but deemed offensive by persons like Malcolm X, who

preferred that words like "Black" be used to describe Black persons of African descent.

"The Caruso Poem" by bill bissett
1. "The Caruso Poem" was written in response to the film *The Great Caruso* (1951), a highly fictionalized biography of Enrico Caruso, the turn-of-the-century world-famous Italian opera singer.

"*From* Dolphins are People" by Milton Acorn
1. "shillelagh" (Line 8) — A thick stick typically used as a weapon.

"Elaboration on a Text" by Milton Acorn
1. This poem is dedicated to Canadian poet Joe Rosenblatt, a friend of Acorn.

"Earnest Word" by Milton Acorn
1. "freedom is the recognition of necessity" (Line 1) — This quotation is from Friedrich Engels and often attributed to German philosopher Georg Wilhelm Friedrich Hegel, an important figure in the philosophical school of German idealism.

"Election Thoughts" by Milton Acorn
1. "little jewman" (Line 21) — This is a derogatory term for a Jewish man.

Editors' Emendations

In Acorn's poems, extra spaces between the end or the start of a word and a punctuation mark have been silently deleted and are not recorded here.

Throughout the text, the roman numerals have been converted to the Arabic numbers to prevent potential confusion.

Lines of poetry that were underlined in the typescript have been converted to italics.

<u>Crossing Directions</u>
20   "Marvel" to "Marvell"

<u>Poem for Sydney</u>
17   "embarressed" to "embarrassed"

<u>The Body</u>
50   "au natural" to "au naturel"

<u>News in a Letter</u>
8   "jeapardy" to "jeopardy"

<u>for Martina</u>
2   "Mazatlan" to "Mazatlán"
3   "nasturium" to "nasturtium"
4   "Telaquepaque" to "Tlaquepaque"

6	"Michoacan" to "Michoacán"	
10	"Zihautenejo" to "Zihuatanejo"	
13	"Chilipancingo" to "Chilpancingo"	

Wouldn't it Be Dreadful
7   "dinasaurs" to "dinosaurs"

Dead Tree
4   "bords" to "birds"

One Day Kennedy Died and So Did the Birdman of Alcatraz
19   "Krushchev's" to "Khrushchev's"

song of a virgins
11   "monigamy" to "monogamy"

Headlights
63   "Chilipancingo" to "Chilpancingo"

suite of five
18   "towell" to "towel"

Man and Daisy at Open Air Meeting
17   "tatoo" to "tattoo"

o where is "and mary" this morning in may if we're all such flowers
12   "sife" to "side"
17   "williamsd" to "william sd"

Khrushchov's Shoe
Title "Khrushchov's" to "Khrushchev's"
1   "Khrushchov's" to "Khrushchev's"

The Fountain
94   "marnle" to "marble"

Earnest Word
Title "Ernest" to "Earnest"

230   Editors' Emendations

Later Publication and Emendation List

The editors acknowledge that due to the ephemeral nature of small press publishing—comprising limited editions, rare broadsides, privately published works, etc.—and accounting for the possibility of lost and damaged works, a complete list of all published versions of both authors' poems is not likely to be achieved.

Unless otherwise stated, a poem's emendations are consistent across all its various publications. In the list of emendations below, the original from *I Want to Tell You Love* appears first.

Abbreviation List for Acorn's Books
Dig Up My Heart – DUMH
The Edge of Home – EH
Hundred Proof Earth – HPE
The Island Means Minago – IMM
In a Springtime Instant – ISI
I've Tasted My Blood – ITMB
Uncollected Acorn – UA

Abbreviation List for bissett's Books
air 1 n 11-12 – AIR
Awake in the Red Desert – ARD
Beyond Even Faithful Legends – BEFL
Nobody Owns th Earth – NOE
Stardust – SD
the jinx ship ad other trips – JST
We sleep inside each other all – WSA

UNTITLED ["LOVER THAT I HOPE YOU ARE ... DO YOU NEED ME?"] by Milton Acorn
Later appeared in *I've Tasted My Blood* (1969), *Dig Up My Heart* (1983), and *In a Springtime Instant* (2012).

4	acceptance,] acceptance
6	manoeuver] manoeuvre
7	armored] armoured (*ISI, DUMH*)
7	knights, with] knights with
16	but once] and who once
16	made the second greatest gamble] made the greatest

AN AFFLICTED MAN'S EXCUSE by Milton Acorn
Later appeared in *I've Tasted My Blood* (1969) and *Dig Up My Heart* (1983).

2	if] If
3	were others] Were others
5	thru my] Thru my
6	, wonderful] Wonderful
6	strange,] strange
7	were going] Were going
8	picking and] Picking up and
9	of which] Of which
9	I say] I say,
10	but what] But what
11	the whole] The whole
11	damn] dam (*ITMB*)
12	into my] Into my
13	my most] My most
14	was universal] Was universal
15	such a precise] Such a precise
16	as to] As to

POEM ["HAIR FLOWING YELLOW AND STILL"] by Milton Acorn
Later appeared in *I've Tasted My Blood* (1969), *Dig Up My Heart* (1983), and *In a Springtime Instant* (2012).

9	collar bone] collarbone	
11	round] around (*ISI*)	

THE SCHOONER by Milton Acorn
Later appeared in *I've Tasted My Blood* (1969), *The Island Means Minago* (1975), *Dig Up My Heart* (1983), *The Edge of Home: Milton Acorn from the Island* (2002), and *In a Springtime Instant* (2012).

3	board,] board; (*IMM*)
7	til,] till, (*ISI, ITMB, DUMH, EH*)
7	til,] til (*IMM*)
7	strong,] strong (*ISI, IT, DUMH, EH*)
8	the wind.] the wind: (*ISI, IT, DUMH, EH*)
9	ways,] ways (*IMM*)
11	darkness;] darkness. (*IMM*)
12	now no] Now no (*IMM*)
13	you but] you, but (*IMM*)

SPARTACUS by Milton Acorn
Later appeared in *Hundred Proof Earth* (1988).

1-3	Never to forgive / a hand with blood / in its fissures,] Never to forgive the hand / with blood worked into its creases,
4-7	not to acknowledge it / his property, but / to peer out / thru the strain creeping] nor to acknowledge / the stink of property / as part of yourself / but to peer out thru / the stain creeping
8	his mindseye] your mind's eye
9	crying] crying,
10	"Look!"] 'Look!' …

11-19	Sparrow pecks [...] the choice of joy.] Not to give in to / the temptation of loyalty / to what you're made to do, / but to forge your own deeds / out of pity and / the will to grow ... // Money also moves / with a half-life / twisting the human / caught in it. / To some this is / freedom, and on it / they build their obligation, / their commitment, / their honour, and / follow it even to death. // My freedom's the uncluttered / eye looking at strength, / and seeing the worm / in its bowels, / seeing the fungus / growing on its tongue.

A CARRIAGE THAT WERE GREEN by bill bissett
Later appeared in *Awake in th red desert* (1968).

59-64	two months [...] has glamour] two months / is plenty / of time // for th mafia's / cornerd / glamour // finally she sd / don't ask for / comfort, pray / for strength

SELF-PORTRAIT by Milton Acorn
Later appeared in *I've Tasted My Blood* (1969), *Dig Up My Heart* (1983), and *In a Springtime Instant* (2012).

1	thank God,] thank God
10	in it] in it.
11	... if they've got] If they have
13	they give] They give
13	In either case] Either way
19	in my] into my

PERFECT by Milton Acorn
Later appeared in *I've Tasted My Blood* (1969) and *Dig Up My Heart* (1983).

5-6	blew / a] blew a
6	smoke-ring!] smoke-ring.
6	Never can do] Never

12	'loving'] "loving"
14-15	thru me: // or I bang] thru me: / or I bang
21	"What did it?"] what did it?
22	me an a] me and a
29	an instant,] an instant
36	held with a] held to with a
38	Whatever it is it lasts ... for] Whatever it is, it's less / and more than the ideal, / which maybe is just me / and also a particularity // : but it lasts ... for
42	carpet.] carpet

THE BODY by bill bissett
Later appeared in *We sleep inside each other all* (1966) and *Beyond Even Faithful Legends, 1962-76* (1980).

2	though] tho (*BEFL*)
3-4	survivors // so] survivors // ... // so (*WSA*)
38	ourselves] ourselvs (*BEFL*)
41	either] eithr (*BEFL*)
41	ourselves] ourselvs (*BEFL*)
46	it was] it is
54	the belief] th belief (*BEFL*)
64	ourselves] ourselvs (*BEFL*)

Additional note: In *I Want to Tell You Love*, "The Body" is typed across three pages (as in the typescript), but the poem was fitted to two pages in *WSA* and BEFL.

POEM FOR A SINGER by Milton Acorn
Later appeared in *I've Tasted My Blood* (1969).

55	ticking ..] ticking ...

THERE IS THE VOODOO IN THE TOWN by bill bissett
Later appeared in *Stardust* (1975).

1-2	in the town / drink it down] in the town drink it down
3	period]
4	law and order] law nd ordr
4	members of a] members uv a
5	are] ar
5	their] ther
5	law and order] law nd ordr
5	commissionaire] commissionair
6	the national harbors board] the Halifax harbors bord
6	the only] th only
7	on the] on th
8	arm of the R C M P] arm uv th r c m p
9	does] duz
10	differ / diffr
10	the animal] th animal
11	does the] duz th
12	differ] diffr
13	the queen] th queen
14	exhibition and] xhibishun nd
15	beetle] beetul
15	of the] uv th
16	night] nite
16	BBC television] bbc televishyun
17	then] thn
17	the] th
17	and] nd
17	heavens] heavns
18	the] th
18	painter] paintr
18	lived] livd
18	everyone] evrywhun
19	the beetles are] th beetuls ar
20	when] whn
21	poem in the] pome in th
23	where] wher

23   be] b

NEWS IN A LETTER by Milton Acorn
Later appeared in *The Uncollected Acorn* (1987).

0	] for Robert Acorn
2	who] Who
3	passions] Passions
5	the pipes] The pipes
5	angle] angle,
6	interfering] Interfering
8	of music] Of music
8	Musician] Musician,
9	sit] Sit
9	Tiger Rag.] *Tiger Rag!*
10	backwards] Backwards
12	and] And
13	be] Be
14	to work with.] To work on.
16	roaring] Roaring
17	might] mighty
18	of] Of
19	then] Then
20	and] And
21-22	joke of / your existence ... live bones in vibration.] joke of your existence, / live bones in vibration.

WE SLEEP INSIDE EACH OTHER ALL by bill bissett
Later appeared in *We sleep inside each other all* (1966).

5-7	i have not yet all the facts / that concern its collapse // the comfort] i have not yet all the facts // the comfort
9	i do] I do
18	he do he joind] he do he joind
27	u] yu

Later Publication and Emendation List   237

POEM ["YOU'LL CLIMB OR FALL FROM THIS MOMENT"]
by Milton Acorn
Later appeared in *I've Tasted My Blood* (1969).

10	a collection] a collective
11	:] ;

POEM FOR THE ASTRONAUTS by Milton Acorn
Later appeared in *I've Tasted My Blood* (1969) and *In a Springtime Instant* (2012).

4	is in the wind] is the wind
9	the eye,] the eye
15	and what] And what
16	the] The

TO CONCEIVE OF TULIPS by Milton Acorn
Later appeared in *I've Tasted My Blood* (1969) and *In a Springtime Instant* (2012).

11	of you not] of not you
13	quieter,] quieter;
14	bowl.] bowl
17	your life, a refuge] your life / a refuge

WHILST WAITING FOR by bill bissett
Later appeared in *Stardust* (1975) and *Beyond Even Faithful Legends, 1962-76* (1980).

17	the] th (*BEFL*)
22	be abul] be / abul (*BEFL*)
23	at luvly] at /luvly (*BEFL*)
25	tree when] tree / when (*BEFL*)
26	the] th (*BEFL*)
26	shud otherwise] shud / otherwise (*BEFL*)
27	kill my eyes] kill / my eyes (*BEFL*)
28	and] and to (*BEFL*)

29	have to put up with those] have to put up / with those (*BEFL*)
30	christians impoverishd] christians / impoverishd (*BEFL*)
31	phony symbolism] phony / symbolism (*BEFL*)
32	they use] they / use (*BEFL*)
33	to keep] to / keep (*BEFL*)
34	pockets full] pockets / full (*BEFL*)
35	parents in th] parents / in th (*BEFL*)
37	century were] century / were (*BEFL*)
37	Ist century] 1st century
40-51	and terribuly ... paranoid at / times] Editor's Note: section moved to centre-left of page in *BEFL*

Additional edits made to this poem in *BEFL*:
1. "a / vampires / song" added to top-right of page
2. The shape of some portions of text, "for [...] beautiful" and "even [...] yu / mind" have been altered which cannot be adequately reflected in these notes.

Additional edits made to this poem in *SD*:
1. The shape of one portion of text, "for [...] beautiful" has been differently altered which cannot be adequately reflected in these notes.

DEAD TREE by Milton Acorn
Later appeared in *The Uncollected Acorn* (1987).

1	blunderzag, dull] blunderzag dull
2	cloud-pockey] cloud-pocked
7-8	he asks: / and why,] he asks: // and why,
11	of the blood. // As if some giant [...] It tickles."] of the blood.

ONE DAY KENNEDY DIED AND SO DID THE BIRDMAN OF ALCATRAZ by Milton Acorn
Later appeared in *I've Tasted My Blood* (1969) and *Dig Up My Heart* (1983).

0	] (Why was Kennedy killed? / He was a rich warmaker / who was beginning to learn / that war didn't pay — / That no people who resisted / him was helpless…/ On / the day he died, murdered / no one will admit knowing / by whom — / Another man / who had done far more good / to the human race, / died; / I wrote this poem —
2	fleck] flick
5-6	they fall // , each one more] they fall / , each one more
36	toilet,] toilet
42	failed.] failed

THUNDER POEM by Milton Acorn
Later appeared in *The Uncollected Acorn* (1987) and *In a Springtime Instant* (2012).

9	Rain;"] Rain";

SUITE OF FIVE by bill bissett
Later appeared in *We sleep inside each other all* (1966) and *Beyond Even Faithful Legends, 1962-76* (1980).

In *I Want to Tell You Love*, "SUITE OF FIVE" is printed across three pages (as in the typescript), but the poem was fitted to two pages in *WSA* and *BEFL*.

POEM ["MY MOTHER GOES IN SLIPPERS"] by Milton Acorn
Later appeared in later appeared in *I've Tasted My Blood* (1969), *The Island Means Minago* (1975), *Dig Up My Heart* (1983), *The Edge of Home: Milton Acorn from the Island* (2002), and *In a Springtime Instant* (2012).

6	tho] though (*IMM*)

7   blossom.] blossom, (*IMM*)

10-14   Now she lives on cigarettes and wine, / goes from potted plant to flower, / knowing the time and manner / of each one's tending.] She had the craftman's pride in her product / and resolved that I should live. / Now I see her thinking with her eyes : / Good…but how good in the end / will take a few more lifetimes to prove. (*IMM*)

THE FOUNTAIN by bill bissett
Later appeared in *We sleep inside each other all* (1966).

22   Peace] peace

Additional note: Section of "The Fountain," beginning with "The general" and ending with "to dust" appear across two pages in *I Want to Tell You Love* but are combined on a single page in *WSA*. Similarly, the section, beginning with "How he resents" and ending with "the fountain." also appears across two pages in *I Want to Tell You Love* but are combined on a single page in *WSA*.

THE TUCSON OWLS by bill bissett
Later appeared in *Nobody Owns th Earth* (1971).

23   trash;artists] trash:artists

DETAIL OF A CITYSCAPE by Milton Acorn
Later appeared in *I've Tasted My Blood* (1969), *Dig Up My Heart* (1983), and *In a Springtime Instant* (2012).

17-18   those / disobedient feet.] those disobedient / feet.

DOES THE NEGRO'S SOFT VOICE by Milton Acorn
Later appeared in *The Uncollected Acorn* (1987) and *In a Springtime Instant* (2012).

7	'oh well' and 'if you were'] "oh well" and "if you were"
7	of it,] of it.
10	Or wear] Or they wear
10	rage] rage,
11	rose on your] rose in your
13	that] That

THE CARUSO POEM by bill bissett
Later appeared in *Awake in th red* desert (1968) and *Stardust* (1975).

0	] summer/'63 – fall/'67 (*ARD*)

> Additional note: Sections of "The Caruso Poem," beginning with "and are later / photographed" and ending with "he uses ether" appear across two pages in *I Want to Tell You Love* but are combined on a single page in *ARD* and *SD*.

FROM DOLPHINS ARE PEOPLE by Milton Acorn
Sections entitled "The Deed" and "No Song" later appeared in *The Uncollected Acorn* (1987)

I. The Deed

5	finger's] fingers'
6	til] till
11	life God crying evil] life, God crying evil,
12	upturning] up-turning

III. No-Song

0	III. No-Song] II. No-Song
6-7	unmusical / for its song;] unmusical for its song;
8	labels] labels;
11	keep] keeps
11	heart:] heart.
17	No Bomb;] No Bomb,
23	yet] Yet

25   I Am] *I Am*

GIRL by Milton Acorn
Later appeared in *I've Tasted My Blood* (1969) and *In a Springtime Instant* (2012).

13   me --- I] me — I

• • •

The following poems by Acorn were later published but were not revised:
1. "The Damnation Machine" later appeared in *I've Tasted My Blood* (1969).
2. "Death Poem" later appeared in *I've Tasted My Blood* (1969), *Dig Up My Heart* (1983), *The Edge of Home: Milton Acorn from the Island* (2002), and *In a Springtime Instant* (2012).
3. "Parting" later appeared in *I've Tasted My Blood* (1969), *Dig Up My Heart* (1983)
4. "Untitled" ["Desire / that's / in me"] later appeared in *I've Tasted My Blood* (1969).
5. "Poem for Sydney" later appeared in *I've Tasted My Blood* (1969), *Dig Up My Heart* (1983), and *In a Springtime Instant* (2012).

The following poem by bissett was later published but not revised:
1. "Headlights" later appeared in *We sleep inside each other all* (1966).

The following poems by bissett could not be verified before the time of publication. Their location in library special collections makes them currently inaccessible:

1. "song uv a virgin" later appeared in *the jinx ship nd other trips* (1966).
2. "two" later appeared in *air 1 n 11-12* (1972).
3. "whn n how ovr high..." later appeared in *the jinx ship nd other trips* (1966)

Index of Poems by Title

Milton Acorn
Adam and Eve as Dancers | 100
An Afflicted Man's Excuse | 77
The Damnation Machine | 151
Dead Tree | 122
Death Poem | 152
Detail of a Cityscape | 157
Does the Negro's Soft Voice | 158
Earnest Word | 180
Elaboration on a Text | 177
Election Thoughts | 182
From Dolphins are People | 171
Girl | 175
Khrushchev's Shoe | 142
The Lost World | 141
Man and Daisy at an Open Air Meeting | 138
The Man in the Iron Mask | 133
News in a Letter | 103
One Day Kennedy Died and So Did the Birdman of Alcatraz | 123
Parting | 111
Perfect | 90
Poem ["Hair flowing yellow and still"] | 79
Poem ["My mother goes in slippers"] | 139
Poem ["You'll climb or fall from this moment"] | 112
Poem for a Singer | 97
Poem for Sydney | 92

Poem for the Astronauts | 115
The Schooner | 82
Self-Portrait | 87
The Slaughter of Innocents | 80
Spartacus | 83
Thunder Poem | 131
To Conceive of Tulips | 117
Two Visions | 114
Untitled ["Desire / that's in / me,"] | 108
Untitled ["Lover that I hope you are … Do you need me?"] | 68
Untitled ["My poor friends. You aren't beautiful"] | 88
Untitled ["The pain corresponds to the leopard's pealing howl"] | 104
Vision in a Quicker Reflection | 107
Wouldn't it Be Dreadful | 118

bill bissett
a carriage that were green | 84
As I Think of Where Today I can Get th Rent Money | 143
The Body | 93
The Caruso Poem | 159
Crossing Directions | 70
for Martina | 113
The Fountain | 145
from five poems for norman mailer | 89
Headlights | 127
Las Palmas | 116
Miracles | 132
o where is "and mary" this morning in may if we're all such flowers | 140
the sand man | 184
song of a virgins | 125
suite of five | 135
there is the voodoo in the town | 101
transparencies | 181
The Tucson Owls | 154
two | 176
Untitled ["asleep on time"] | 81
we sleep inside each other all | 109
when and how over high mountain into high dream out | 105
whilst waiting for | 120

Acknowledgements

It was on 23 September 2010 that Eric Schmaltz, shortly after learning about *I Want to Tell You Love*'s existence and whereabouts, asked bill bissett if he would like to see it published one day. bissett turned to him and said, "you really just need a printer to publish a book of poems." Though bissett is correct, the work that has gone into this edition of *I Want to Tell You Love* far exceeds the task of printing a book, and it is the result of a multitude of friends, colleagues, archivists, librarians, and supporters who shared their time and knowledge through discussion, teaching, reports, correspondence, and late-night phone calls and instant messaging. We want to express our deep appreciation to everyone who has supported the project along the way. We are grateful to bill bissett. This project would not have been possible without bill's love, generosity, and belief in us. We are grateful, too, to Mary Hooper, the former literary executor to Milton Acorn's estate, who graciously granted us permission to carry out this project. We valued her support, correspondence, and kindness as we worked on this book. This book also would not have been possible without the guidance of Gregory Betts, who first alerted Eric to the typescript in Acorn's archive at Library and Archives Canada in Ottawa. This edition grows directly out of Gregory's many forms of support for this project. Other scholars, poets, colleagues, friends, and publishers have had a significant and direct impact on this book including James Allard, Sydney Anne, Kathy Armstrong, derek beaulieu, Jim Brown, Stephen Cain, Rose Crawford, Jeremy Colangelo, Tim Conley, Andrew Connolly, Melissa Dalgleish, Siobhan Doody, Chris Faiers, Beatriz Hausner, Lesley

Higgins, Dean Irvine, J. Douglas Kneale, J. M. Huculak, Karl Jirgens, Shannon Maguire, Donato Mancini, Seymour Mayne, Jay Millar, Hazel Millar, Philip Miletic, Shane Neilson, Zailig Pollock, Alysha Puopolo, Raymond Souster, and our peer-reviewers whose insight and expertise shaped this edition. The editors are also indebted to the significant work of librarians and archivists at Library and Archives Canada, the James A. Gibson Library at Brock University, Thomas Fisher Special Collections at the University of Toronto, and Clara Thomas Special Collections at York University. We extend a very special thank you to Anna St. Onge at York University for helping us solve some of the mysteries surrounding the typescripts. We are also grateful to the various forms of institutional support that we received while working on this edition. We extend our gratitude to Editing Modernism in Canada, whose scholarly network and gatherings provided much of the groundwork for this edition. Thank you to preeminent journal *Canadian Literature* for publishing Schmaltz's early scholarship on *I Want to Tell You Love*, some of which has been revised and included in the Introduction to this book. We are also grateful for the direct support given to this project through the Social Sciences and Humanities Research Council, Clara Thomas Doctoral Scholarship in Canadian Studies, and the Kenneth Frederick White Memorial Graduate Scholarship. Reprint rights for some of Acorn's poems were purchased from Mosaic Press. Credit is due to the generous persons who assisted in providing the funding needed to secure permissions for a number of these poems that are also included in *In a Springtime Instant* (Mosaic, 2012). The editors extend their thanks to the donors of the Linda Heather Lamont-Stewart Scholarship in Canadian Literature at York for their financial support to pay for these reprint rights. Finally, thank you to everybody at the University of Calgary Press for supporting this project and all the hard work done on its behalf—especially Alison Cobra, Melina Cusano, Kyle Flemmer, Helen Hajnoczky, and Brian Scrivener.

Index

A

Abrams, M. H., 45
Acorn, Milton: birth of, 19; career of, 4-5, 19, 21; carpenter, 19, 28, 191; death of, 5, 190; Governor General's Award, 4-5, 22; Gwendolyn MacEwen (*see* MacEwen, Gwendolyn); in Vancouver, 4, 17, 19, 20, 22, 31, 42, 50, 52, 190; People's Poet, 1, 5, 23; in Prince Edward Island, 19, 22, 190; personality of, 20, 23, 49-50; poems (*see* Index of Poems by Title, 245-246); rules for poetry, 23; in Toronto, 19-23, 190
— books of: *Against a League of Liars*, 20; *The Brain's the Target*, 19, 20, 41, 43; *Dig Up My Heart, Selected Poems, 1952-83*, 34; *I Shout Love and On Shaving Off His Beard*, 50; *The Island Means Minago*, 5; *I've Tasted My Blood*, 4, 5, 22, 34, 42, 50; *In Love and Anger*, 3, 20, 30, 43; *Jawbreakers*, 20
— contributions to: *Georgia Straight, The*, 17, 21; *Moment*, 21, 25
— poems discussed throughout book: "An Afflicted Man's Excuse," 34; "AVOID THE BAD MOUNTAIN," 23, 41; "Charlottetown Harbour," 41; "The Damnation Machine," 34, 43; "Detail of a Cityscape," 34, 43; "Earnest Word," 43; "I Shout Love," 50; "One Day Kennedy Died and So Did the Birdman of Alcatraz," 43; "Poem for a Singer," 34, 46; "Poem for Sydney," 194-195; "The Schooner," 34, 42; "Wouldn't it Be Dreadful," 37
Advance Mattress Coffee House. *See under* Vancouver
American Influence, 6, 8, 10-11, 13, 22
Atwood, Margaret, 10, 22-23, 26; *Survival*, 10
avant-garde, 1, 4-6, 25-26, 30, 35-37, 45, 48-49, 51-52
Avison, Margaret, 13, 26, 29

B

Barthes, Roland, 37
Bataille, Georges, 44
Baudelaire, Charles, 3
Berrigan, Ted, 26
Betts, Gregory, 4, 35
Birney, Earle, 12, 24, 26, 33
bissett, bill: birth of, 24; career of, 3, 5, 25, 29, 53, 191; daughter (Michelle), 26, 28, 187, 192, 215, 218; in Halifax, 24; at the Mandan Ghetto, 26; radical poetry of, 3-5, 27, 34-35, 38, 40, 46, 50-52; Martina Clinton's relationship with, 25, 26, 28, 187, 192, 216, 218; poems (*see* Index of Poems by Title, 247); sexuality of, 24, 26-27; in *Strange Grey Day This*, 24; in Toronto, 5, 24, 34, 51, 189, 198; trip to Mexico and the United States, 28, 30, 187-188, 192, 218; in Vancouver, 17, 24-28, 191-192
— *blewointment press*, 5, 14, 15, 17, 25-26, 28, 33, 187, 197; renamed Nightwood Editions, 51;

251

pornography claims against, 5, 51;
What Isint Tantrik Speshul, 28
— books of: *Fires in th tempul OR th jinx ship nd othr trips*, 3, 5, 26; *We Sleep Inside Each Other All*, 3, 5, 26, 34
— poems discussed throughout book: "a carriage that were green," 47; "suite of five," 34; "Th Canadian," 23, 193; "The Body," 29, 34, 40, 46, 193, 198; "The Fountain," 34; "The Tucson Owls," 214; "we sleep inside each other all," 34; "when and how over high mountain into high dream out," 39
Blake, William, 45-46
blewointment press. *See under* bissett, bill
Bowering, George, 12-13, 22, 26, 31, 45-46
Brazilia 73, 26
Britain, 6, 9
Brown, Jim, 33
Bullock, Ruth, 18, 191
Butling, Pauline, 10

C

Călinescu, Matei, 36, 48
Canada Council for the Arts, 9, 46
Canadian Forum, 29, 198
Canadian Literature, 4-5, 9-10, 30, 50, 53
Canadian Literature (Journal), 9
Canadian Tribune, 43
Cellar Jazz Club. *See under* Vancouver
Charlottetown, 19
Civil Rights Movement, 2, 7-8, 225
Clinton, Martina. *See under* bissett, bill
Cobbing, Bob, 26
Cogswell, Fred, 2, 32. *See also Fiddlehead*
Communism, 8, 35, 37, 43, 45, 221. *See also* Marxism
"Conclusion to a *Literary History of Canada*" (Frye, Northrop), 10
consciousness, 36-39, 44-45, 48, 51, 193
Copithorne, Judith, 11, 14-16, 25, 38, 192-193
counterculture, 1-2, 4, 15, 17, 19-21, 26-27, 48-51. *See also under* Vancouver
Coupey, Pierre, 21, 22, 26
Creeley, Robert, 13

D

Dart, Ron, 6-7
Davey, Frank, 11-13
Diefenbaker, John, 6
downtown poets. *See under* Vancouver
Doyle, James, 35, 42, 43
Duncan, Robert, 13

E

Expo 67, 10

F

Farrell, Lance, 25, 56n38, 191
Fiddlehead, 20, 32-33, 50. *See also* Cogswell, Fred

G

Gadd, Maxine, 14, 16, 38, 51, 187, 192, 193
Ginsberg, Allen, 13-14
Governor General's Award, 51. *See also under* Acorn, Milton
Gudgeon, Chris, 18

I

I Want to Tell You Love: attempts to publish, 2, 4-5, 22, 31-33, 38, 53, 191, 213; collaboration on, 2, 24, 28, 30-31, 34, 48-49, 191, 193-194, 197, 213; experimental approach to, 4, 35, 38-40, 193; typescript, 3, 4, 29-30, 33, 35, 38, 40, 46, 52, 54n1, 213-214
Innis, Harold Adams, 37

J

Jankola, Beth, 192-193
Jewinski, Ed, 18, 28, 50

K

Karasick, Adeena, 3, 198
Kearns, Lionel, 13, 51
Keats, John, 45
Kennedy, John F., 2, 6, 43, 221
Kerouac, Jack, 26
Kiyooka, Roy, 14, 16, 26
Kostelanetz, Richard, 26

L

Lane, Patrick, 21, 28, 192-193
Lane, Red, 21-22
League of Canadian Poets, 32
Lee, Dennis, 7, 10; *Civil Elegies*, 10
Lemm, Richard, 18, 21
levy, d. a., 26
Livesay, Dorothy, 12, 16-17, 23, 26, 38, 41, 46
love, 21, 38, 44-45, 49-50, 52-53, 193-194, 196
Lowther, Pat, 12, 16-17, 21, 24, 26, 38, 187, 192-193

M

MacEwen, Gwendolyn, 19-22, 50, 56n48
Malcolm X, 28, 225, 226
Marxism, 8, 18, 19, 35, 43. *See also* Communism
Massey Report, The, 8
McCaffery, Steve, 3, 26, 51
McLuhan, Marshall, 15, 37
Moment. See under Acorn, Milton
Montreal, 10, 19
mosaic, 34, 36-38, 40, 44, 46, 48-49, 52
Moss, Laura, 7
Mount, Nick, 9-10

N

national identity, 6-10, 13, 15
Neil, Al, 14, 16
Neilson, Shane, 3, 35
New American Poetry, 1945-1960, The (Allen, Donald), 13
Nichol, bp, 25-26, 34, 51

O

Olson, Charles, 13, 50

P

People's Poet. *See under* Acorn, Milton
Persky, Stan, 21
poems. *See* Index of Poems by Title, 245-247
Poggioli, Renato, 36
PRISM magazine, 39
Purdy, Al, 12, 16, 18-23, 26, 35, 41-42, 45-46, 50

R

radicalism, 4, 16, 18, 34-38, 42, 45-46, 48, 50, 188
Rankin, J. A., 2-3, 31-33
Reid, Jamie, 8, 12-14, 16, 27, 193; *A Temporary Stranger*, 14
revolution, 2, 4, 20, 35-36, 45-46, 48-50
Richler, Mordecai, 22
Rimbaud, Arthur, 36, 52
Rosenblatt, Joe, 23, 227
Russell, Charles, 48

S

Scobie, Stephen, 26
Shelley, Percy, 45-47
socialism, 15, 18, 21, 42, 50, 216
Souster, Raymond, 2, 32-33, 188-189, 192
Sugars, Cynthia, 7
Sullivan, Rosemary, 19-20, 50

T

Tallman, Ellen, 14
Tallman, Warren, 12-14, 16, 22, 24, 30, 46
TISH. *See under* Vancouver
Toronto, 5, 9-10, 11, 19-23, 197; Bohemian Embassy, 9, 19; Ward's Island, 20
Toronto Daily Star, 9
Toronto Harbourfront Reading Series, 10
Turner, Michael, 16

U

United States, 2, 6-9, 195, 218, 221, 222, 224
University of British Columbia (UBC), 12-14, 16-17, 21, 24

V

Vancouver, 4-6, 11-12, 14-22, 24-28, 31, 34, 37-38, 42, 47, 50, 52-53, 187, 190-192; 1960s, 11, 15-17, 21, 26, 37; Advance Mattress Coffee House, 21, 29, 38, 196; Acorn and bissett in, 5-6, 17-18, 187, 191; Cellar Jazz Club, 14, 16, 27, 192-193; downtown poets, 14, 16, 23-24;

Index 253

literary scene, 12, 14-17, 21-22, 24, 38, 53; counterculture in, 4, 20, 26, 50; League of Socialist Action, 18; TISH, 12, 14-17, 22-24, 38; Vanguard Books, 15, 18, 21, 28, 29, 38, 187, 191, 192, 193
Vancouver Poetry Conference, 13
Vancouver School of Art, 14
Vancouver Sun, 21
Vanguard Books. *See under* Vancouver
Very Stone House, 31-33, 52
Vietnam War, 2, 8-9, 36, 187, 193, 195, 224

W

Wah, Fred, 12-13
Wershler, Darren, 3
Whitman, Walt, 46
Wiesenthal, Christine, 16; *The Half-Lives of Pat Lowther*, 16
Wordsworth, William, 45, 47
Writers' Union of Canada, The, 10

www.ingramcontent.com/pod-product-compliance
Lightning Source LLC
Chambersburg PA
CBHW061254230426
43665CB00027B/2940